The Land and People of

THE NETHERLANDS

Published Portraits of the Nations Books

The Land and People of Afghanistan

The Land and People of Argentina

The Land and People of Bolivia

The Land and People of Cambodia

The Land and People of Canada

The Land and People of China

The Land and People of Finland

The Land and People of France

The Land and People of Kenya

The Land and People of Korea

The Land and People of Malaysia and Brunei

The Land and People of Mongolia

The Land and People of The Netherlands

The Land and People of Scotland

The Land and People of South Africa

The Land and People of The Soviet Union

The Land and People of Turkey

The Land and People of Venezuela

The Land and People of Zimbabwe

The Land and People of®
THE NETHERLANDS

by *Theo van Stegeren*

HarperCollins*Publishers*

To Vera

Country maps by Philip Stickler/Stickler Cartography

Every effort has been made to locate the copyright holders
of all copyrighted materials and secure the necessary permission
to reproduce them. In the event of any questions arising as
to their use, the publisher will be glad to make necessary
changes in future printings and editions.

The Land and People of The Netherlands
Copyright © 1991 by HarperCollins Publishers
Printed in the U.S.A. All rights reserved.
For information address HarperCollins Children's Books, a division of
HarperCollins Publishers, 10 East 53rd Street, New York, NY 10022
1 2 3 4 5 6 7 8 9 10
First Edition

Library of Congress Cataloging-in-Publication Data
Stegeren, Theo van.
  The land and people of The Netherlands / by Theo van
Stegeren.
      p.   cm.—(Portraits of the nations)
  Includes bibliographical references and index.
  Summary: Introduces the land, the people, the economy, and
the government of the Netherlands.
  ISBN 0-06-022537-8. — ISBN 0-06-022538-6 (lib. bdg.)
  1. Netherlands—Juvenile literature.   [1. Netherlands.]
I. Title. II. Series.
DJ18.S84 1991   90-47650
949.2—dc20   CIP
                                                   AC

Contents

World Map: *Robinson Projection*   viii

Mini Facts   x

I   The Dutch   1

Privacy and Contact; Class, Clothes, and Cars; Leveling and
Restraint; Taboo on Private Wealth; Ethics; Deviance and Tolerance;
Adapting to Change; Pluralism and Freedom; Preacher and Merchant

Map: *Political Map of the Netherlands*   xii
Chart: *Population Density*   6

II   Land and Water   21

Landscape Types; Soil; Flora and Fauna; Water and History; Water
as Enemy; Land Reclamation; Zuiderzee and Barrier Dam; The
Deltaplan

Boxes: *The Provinces*   29
        Land and Water in Literature   32
        Turning Water Into Land   41
Maps: *Six Landscapes*   27
        Reclaiming the Land   35

III   A First Impression   49

The Morning; At School; At Home; Food and Celebration; Dutch
Traditions; A Typical Home

Boxes: *The Weather: Changeable*   52
        At Home in Holland and America   58
        The Immigrants and Their Children   62
        The Celebration of Sinterklaasfeest   65

IV   Early History   68

The Romans; Charlemagne; The Burgundian Empire; Church
Reformation; William of Orange; Antwerp Falls: A Republic Is Born;
Expansion Overseas; Trade in the West; Slavery
Boxes: *Time Line*   70
      The Dutch Language   74
      The Gothic Style   82
      Amsterdam, Center of the World   92
      Tulip Mania   95
Maps: *The Netherlands Two Thousand Years Ago*   73
     The Eighty Years War   86
     Dutch Exploration and Trade   93

V   The Golden Age   97

The Age of Erasmus; Protest and Dissension; Fear and Piety; The
Thinkers; The Masters
Boxes: *The Spirit of Freedom*   100
      National Sin   111

VI   Modern History   114

Political Crisis; King of the Netherlands; A New Constitution;
Abraham Kuyper and His Ordinary People; World War II; The
Jewish Tragedy; The Resistance; The Last Winter; Loss of Colonies
Box: *Max Havelaar*   123

VII   An Amazing Economy   138

Church and Commerce; Economic Recovery; Cooperation; Export;
The World's Busiest Port; Industry and Agriculture; To Spend or
to Save
Box: *The Big Three*   147
Chart: *The Dutch: Where Do and Did They Work?*   139

VIII   Double Democracy   153

Kings and Queens; Elections and Coalitions; To Vote or Not to Vote;
Verzuiling; Action Groups; Protest and Harmony
Box: *Monarchy*   157

IX Welfare and Justice   168

The Welfare System; Black Money; No Ghettos; Prisons; Abortion,
Euthanasia, Drugs
Box: *The Desire for a Middle Way*   171
Chart: *Spending by the Central Government*   169

X Leisure, Sports, and Arts   186

Sports; Soccer; Skating; Television and Other Media; The Decline of
a Unique Broadcasting Structure; Arts
Box: *Dutch Artists Abroad*   203

XI Holland's Future   206

Poisoned Environment; The European Community

Bibliography   211

Filmography   215

Index   217

THE WORLD

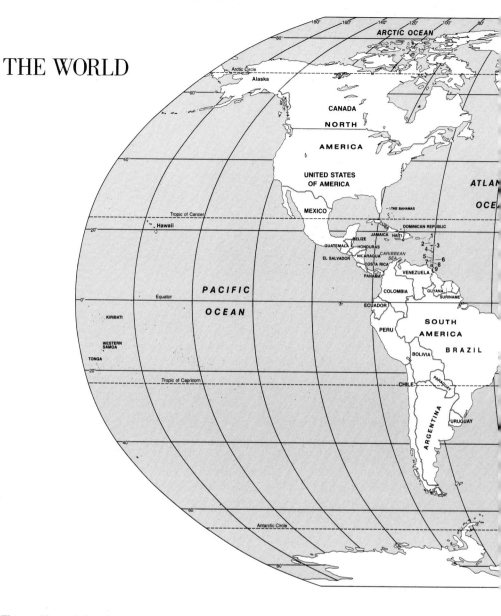

This world map is based on a projection developed by Arthur H. Robinson. The shape of each country and its size, relative to other countries, are more accurately expressed here than in previous maps. The map also gives equal importance to all of the continents, instead of placing North America at the center of the world. *Used by permission of the Foreign Policy Association.*

Legend

—— International boundaries

-------- Disputed or undefined boundaries

Projection: Robinson

0	1000	2000	3000 Miles
0	1000	2000	3000 Kilometers

Caribbean Nations

1. Anguilla
2. St. Christopher and Nevis
3. Antigua and Barbuda
4. Dominica
5. St. Lucia
6. Barbados
7. St. Vincent
8. Grenada
9. Trinidad and Tobago

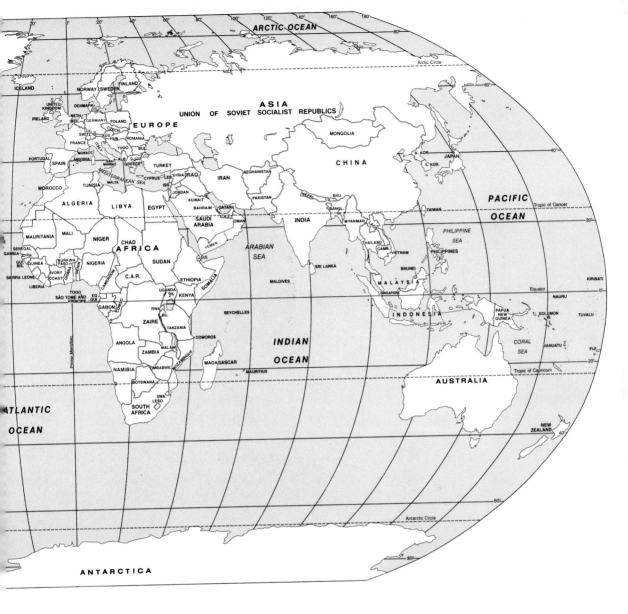

Abbreviations

ALB.	—Albania	C.A.R.	—Central African Republic	LEB.	—Lebanon	SWA.	—Swaziland
AUS.	—Austria	CZECH.	—Czechoslovakia	LESO.	—Lesotho	SWITZ.	—Switzerland
BANGL.	—Bangladesh	DJI.	—Djibouti	LIE.	—Liechtenstein	U.A.E.	—United Arab Emirates
BEL.	—Belgium	EQ. GUI.	—Equatorial Guinea	LUX.	—Luxemburg	YUGO.	—Yugoslavia
BHU.	—Bhutan	GER.	Germany	NETH.	—Netherlands		
BU.	—Burundi	GUI. BIS.	—Guinea Bissau	N. KOR.	—North Korea		
BUL.	—Bulgaria	HUN.	—Hungary	RWA.	—Rwanda		
CAMB.	—Cambodia	ISR.	—Israel	S. KOR.	—South Korea		

Mini Facts

OFFICIAL NAME: Kingdom of the Netherlands *(Koninkrijk der Nederlanden)*

LOCATION: Situated in northwestern Europe, with the North Sea to the west and the north, Belgium to the south, Germany to the east.

AREA: 13,967 square miles (36,184 square kilometers)

HIGHEST POINT: Vaalserberg: 1,053 feet (321 meters)

LOWEST POINT: Near Rotterdam: -22 feet (-6.7 meters)

CAPITAL: Amsterdam

CENTER OF GOVERNMENT: The Hague

POPULATION: 15,000,000 (1990 est.)

MAJOR LANGUAGE: Dutch

RELIGIONS: Roman Catholicism, Protestantism, Islam, Judaism

TYPE OF GOVERNMENT: Monarchy

HEAD OF STATE: Queen

HEAD OF GOVERNMENT: Prime Minister

PARLIAMENT: The States General, or parliament, consists of two houses: the Upper House (75 members, 4-year terms), and the Lower House (150 members, 4-year terms)

ADULT LITERACY: 98 percent

LIFE EXPECTANCY: Female, 76; Male, 70.3 (1988)

MAIN PRODUCTS: *Agriculture*—dairy products, vegetables, beef, pork, sugar beets, potatoes, flowers, seeds, cereal grains. *Manufacturing and processing*—oil and gas products, chemicals, steel products, electronic and telecommunications equipment, machines, automobiles. *Mining and drilling*—natural gas, oil, salt.

MONETARY UNIT: Guilder or *gulden*; $1 = 1.65 guilders

England

THE
NETHERLANDS

Belgium Germany

France

North Sea

GERMANY

BELGIUM

Wadden Sea

GRONINGEN

Groningen

Leeuwarden

FRIESLAND

Assen

DRENTHE

OVERIJSSEL

Zwolle

Almelo

Hengelo

Enschede

Deventer

Barrier Dam

Den Helder

NORTH
HOLLAND

Alkmaar

*IJsselmeer
(Zuiderzee)*

IJssel

*NORTH
SEA*

Haarlem

Amsterdam

Amstelveen

Hilversum

GELDERLAND

Amersfoort

Apeldoorn

Leiden

Utrecht

The Hague

*GREEN
HEART*

Arnhem

SOUTH
HOLLAND

UTRECHT

Rhine

Delft

Schiedam

Europoort

Rotterdam

Vlaardingen

Waal

Nijmegen

GERMANY

Rhine

Dordrecht

Maas

's Hertogenbosch

Westerschelde

Middelburg

ZEELAND

Oosterschelde

Breda

Tilburg

NORTH
BRABANT

Helmond

Eindhoven

Venlo

BELGIUM

LIMBURG

Heerlen

Maastricht

THE NETHERLANDS

—··— International boundaries

——— Provincial boundaries

 Towns with more than 100,000 inhabitants

● Towns with 50,000-100,000 inhabitants

● Towns with 20,000-50,000 inhabitants

· Towns with 10,000-20,000 inhabitants

0	10	20	30	40	50 km
0		10		20	30 miles

The Dutch

Picture someone watching television in North America. Every day this person sees news programs featuring the superpowers and the control they wield over the oceans and the continents. Holland is hardly ever mentioned. Most people cannot imagine that there was a time when Holland was one of those superpowers. Yet three centuries ago Holland was the "Japan" of the world and other nations followed its activities with a mixture of admiration and envy.

For someone visiting Holland—or the Netherlands, as it is officially named—this contradiction between past and present is less puzzling. Well-preserved warehouses, ports, churches, and houses throughout the country are reminders of the "Golden" seventeenth century, an era in which the Dutch established settlements on every continent. And mod-

Canal in Amsterdam with houseboats and waterbikes. Photo by ANP

ern Netherlanders carry on their ancestors' tradition of world citizenship. They travel a lot and, in addition to Dutch, most speak English, many speak German, and some speak French. They are well informed about foreign countries and still make an effort to exert an influence on world affairs.

Officially only the western part of the country is called Holland. In common usage, however, the names Holland and the Netherlands are alternately used to indicate the entire country. The Netherlands—literally, the lowlands—is bounded by the North Sea to the north and west, by Belgium to the south and west, and by Germany to the east.

The land is for the most part flat, its soil fertile. One would hardly notice that Holland is the second most densely populated area in the world; its 15 million inhabitants are pretty evenly distributed across the country. There are not that many skyscrapers in the cities, and even the busiest regions are surrounded by green fields. On the other hand, every square foot of Dutch land has been considered for one use or another. And the highways are rarely quiet. Together with Japan, Holland possesses more cars per square mile and accumulates more car miles per person than any other country in the world. On average the Dutch drive twice as many miles as the citizens of the United States.

Water is the source of much of Holland's wealth and welfare. And yet it has been the nation's greatest challenge. Bordered by the sea and crisscrossed by rivers, Holland has been able to prosper from fishing

River landscape in central Holland. The strips of land between dike and river are used as fields, pastures, or orchards. Photo from Cas Oorthuys archive

and foreign trade. In the western part of Holland, which lies mainly below sea level, water is never far away. Cities are intersected by canals; many towns are located along waterways, lakes, or rivers. Fishermen earn their livings at sea, while in the background big tankers can be seen making their way toward Dutch ports. Rivers serve as passageways for lines of cargo ships; canals sometimes function as streets and provide space for people living on houseboats.

But the sea has also brought destruction. Finding ways to control it has preoccupied people living in the low countries for thousands of years.

This book about Holland begins with a description of its inhabitants, the Dutch. After all, they are the people who have managed to protect the land effectively against the wind and sea, who have made Holland the free and prosperous land that it is today.

Privacy and Contact

In the eyes of some foreign visitors, Dutch life seems highly organized and cultured. Rentes de Carvalho, a Portuguese diplomat, observed in 1987 that

the telephones [are] efficient, ships are guided by radar, computers do the administrative work; yet those expecting romance and adventure around every corner will instead catch a cold. The visitor will encounter millions of individuals who are not in for fantasies, for losing time, for carelessness, not to mention indolence, keen as they are on planning, programming, and structuring.

People visiting Holland for the first time often complain that it is difficult to get to know the Dutch. Most Netherlanders refrain from conversation, unless unavoidable, with someone they do not know. An Italian writer once remarked that the Dutch, in contrast with his own compatriots, speak only when they have something to say.

On a train, for example, most people will try to find a seat located as far from others as possible. Passengers remain silent and try to avoid other people's glances. This reserve arises from the Dutch desire not to intrude upon one another's privacy. According to one American observer, this is how Dutch travelers manage to avoid contact on public transportation. If you are one of the first to enter the vehicle, spread your belongings out across the adjoining seat(s). Then stretch your legs out to block access to vacant seats. The rule is, sit in the aisle seat when the window seat is not occupied. If someone comes along looking for

Population Density

China
(1050 million inhabitants)
■ ■ ■ ■ ■
■ ■ ■ ■ ■
■

Brazil
(143 million inhabitants)
■

United States
(241 million inhabitants)
■ ■

Japan
(121 million inh.)
■ ■ ■ ■ ■
■ ■ ■ ■ ■
■ ■ ■ ■ ■
■ ■ ■ ■ ■
■ ■ ■ ■ ■
■ ■ ■ ■ ■
■

France
(55 million inh.)
■ ■ ■ ■ ■
■ ■ ■ ■ ■

Hungary
(11 million inh.)
■ ■ ■ ■ ■
■ ■ ■ ■ ■
■ ■

Nigeria
(105 million inh.)
■ ■ ■ ■ ■
■ ■ ■ ■ ■

The Netherlands
(15.6 million inh.)
■ ■ ■ ■ ■
■ ■ ■ ■ ■
■ ■ ■ ■ ■
■ ■ ■ ■ ■
■ ■ ■ ■ ■
■ ■ ■ ■ ■
■ ■ ■ ■ ■
■ ■ ■ ■ ■
■

■ 10 persons per km²
Population density in a number of countries. The Netherlands is one of the most densely populated countries in the world with 402.9 people per square km.

a place to sit, ignore him/her by looking away, reading a newspaper, or pretending to be asleep. The Dutch normally see no reason for bothering other people. But given a legitimate cause, that silence will quickly be broken. When a dispute breaks out between two train passengers, one can be sure that the rest of the car will soon burst out into a lively chatter.

Add to this the Dutch difficulty in expressing emotions and it may become clear why some strangers find social life in Holland so depressing. The same Portuguese diplomat mentioned above remarked, "What strikes me here is the solemnity, the gloom, the saddening certainty that the conversation will inevitably be about God, politics, or the cost of living."

This inner restraint explains why the Dutch are not accustomed to making good friends quickly. They certainly have their acquaintances, but intimacy for them doesn't go much further than drinking a sociable cup of coffee. The Dutch are most at ease when they are *gezellig thuis.* *Thuis* is the Dutch word for "at home." *Gezellig* is a favorite word in Holland, loosely translated as "cozy," cozy as a conversation with family and close friends. Birthdays, Christmases, and New Year's Eves rank highest among these days of intimacy and informality. On such evenings grandparents, aunts, uncles, nieces, and nephews drop by and gather in the living room. While several rounds of coffee are being served, preferably with cake or pastry, they talk about illnesses in the family and the children's achievements in school. Later in the evening, when beer, wine, and whiskey are placed on the table, an uncle starts telling jokes, while others debate politics or religion. The children, allowed to stay up longer, play games or watch television, amply stocked with candy, lemonade, cookies, peanuts, and chips.

One of the evenings with a high degree of *gezelligheid* (coziness) is New Year's Eve. People stay at home with family or friends and eat

The quiet side of Holland: windmill near Hoofddorp, North Holland. Photo by Theo van Stegeren

apple turnovers and *oliebollen* (a kind of doughnut ball), covered with soft sugar. For almost thirty years New Year's Eve in the Netherlands regularly included the radio appearances of Wim Kan (1911–1983), a cabaret performer who, listened to by a massive audience, gave his satirical views on the past year and on controversial current affairs. From 1973 until he died in 1983, he continued the tradition on television.

For Wim Kan nothing and nobody was sacred. With great wit, brilliant wordplay, and a fine sense of timing, he criticized everyone, radical or conservative, Roman Catholic or Protestant. But he did more than that. One moment he could make the Prime Minister or the Pope look a fool, and the next moment he could put his audience into a reflective, even somber mood by singing about his experiences in the war—he spent most of World War II in a Japanese concentration camp—or about the problem of mercy killing.

Sometimes people felt offended by his mockery, but that did not harm his national popularity at all. He gave the Dutch people—whom he once affectionately described as "fourteen million doughnut balls in a frying pan, heated by natural gas"—a feeling of togetherness. He symbolized their "agreement to disagree" and made them feel proud of their tolerance of each other's views and habits. And perhaps most important, he raised controversial issues, which stimulated difficult discussions and led people to take moral stands.

Class, Clothes, and Cars

Viewed in a crowd, the Dutch tend to be rather tall and their hair is often blond. There is, however, a substantial non-white minority. People look healthy and strong. The way they interact with each other is noticeably direct, marked by close eye-to-eye contact and a rather formal interchange. One gets the feeling that these people are getting right down to the business at hand.

More difficult to determine at first glance is the social rank or position to which people belong. Extravagant clothing is uncommon, yet one would be hard put to find someone dressed shabbily. The vast majority of people—be they rich or poor—are dressed in casual, rather unimaginative clothes. People do get spruced up for a party, disco, or theater, but a glamorous look is the exception. Because Dutch ecologists have targeted issues involving cruelty to animals, fur coats are considered inappropriate.

Likewise, extremes are avoided in the choice of cars. Limousines and high-priced cars are few and far between on Dutch highways, but with

The busy side of Holland: traffic jam.   Photo by Rijkswaterstaat

the introduction of mandatory inspection, aged or run-down cars are just as difficult to find. Most Dutch people drive medium-sized, medium-priced cars. It takes a sensitive observer to detect the subtle differences between the various social groups and classes in the Netherlands.

Leveling and Restraint

At this point, one typical characteristic of the Dutch may be apparent: They are wary of extremes. "Act normal, and you'll be conspicuous enough" is still a much-heard remark in Holland. Regardless of whether you're a leading rock star, executive, or politician, you'd better try to behave like everyone else. If you don't, your popularity will suffer. "Somehow she's just remained the ordinary girl she always was" is the most flattering comment a Dutch movie star can receive. Even at school, a student who grows too achievement oriented will quickly fall victim to the mockery of his or her classmates.

One Dutch author, Godfried Bomans, described this Dutch trait this way:

We don't like someone to be much lower than ourselves, but we also don't want them to be much higher. Anything that rises above its surroundings arouses the urge in us to level it. This primitive drive to level others is already present in our children at an early stage. When children graffiti the fence with the statement "John is crazy," it doesn't mean that John is insane. If that were the case, we would have immediately established a fund-raising campaign. What it actually means is that John behaves conspicuously, and that's something he shouldn't do.

The Dutch are too commonsensical to let themselves get carried away with their emotions. Close friends kiss each other on the cheek when they meet each other, but often in a rather awkward way. Netherlanders give each other presents, but these gifts are modest: Flowers or books are common. An expensive gift may be embarrassing to the receiver. The Dutch desire for a happy medium is one sign of the lingering influence of Calvinism, particularly in the northern half of the country. One of the stricter forms of Protestantism, Calvinism holds that people naturally tend to lead sinful lives. People can receive the grace of God by totally surrendering to Him and by accepting the Bible as the only source of all rules for living and believing. Calvinists, then, lead a life of self-control and restraint. Although the power of Calvinism is diminishing in Holland, and the virtues that it has preached are no longer taken for granted everywhere, its traces are still clearly present.

Taboo on Private Wealth

Since Holland is one of the economic centers of the world, a discussion of money is central to any picture of the Netherlands. Multinational companies like Shell, Unilever, Philips, DSM (Dutch State Mines), and Akzo Group are based in Holland. Rotterdam is the busiest port in the world. After Japan, Holland is the world's largest investor in foreign countries.

Yet in the Netherlands many avoid talking about money, particularly a person's private financial affairs. Inquiring about the size of some-one's private income is taboo. This taboo extends throughout all layers of society. The assets of the Dutch royal family are estimated to be worth several hundred millions of dollars, but no one really has any idea of the exact amount. The royal family itself remains silent on this matter. Supposed to be above politics, the family does not want to reveal its financial ties and interests. Full disclosure could harm its image of impartiality. Yet the attitude of the Queen and her family also reflects the embarrassment all Dutch people feel about showing or admitting their private wealth.

Since the Middle Ages, people in the Netherlands have read the Bible as teaching them to spend their money wisely. One shouldn't throw money away; someone who possesses great wealth should give a portion to those less fortunate. Later in the nineteenth and twentieth centuries, Dutch socialists lent their weight to this view. Socialists blame the "capitalists"—the owners of factories, raw materials, and machines— for the existence of injustice and poverty. They see a social revolution that would give workers a greater role in owning and controlling indus-try as the only way to a happy, classless society. Although socialism has not shaped Dutch thinking to the same degree as has Christianity, it has encouraged the belief that wealth is inherently evil: Someone with a lot of money must have earned it by taking advantage of others, at home or elsewhere in the world.

Ethics

Centuries of Christianity and decades of socialism have made the Dutch deeply aware of their own consciences. Netherlanders have become specialists in ethical matters. Nothing can stop them from taking a position and swinging into action, particularly when the suffering of people or animals is at stake. "Action groups" are set up; demonstrations are organized. Ethical questions are examined in long and serious discussions. In the late 1980's, questions concerning collaboration during World War II and the punishment of former Nazis were still being debated nationwide. Abortion and euthanasia have been central issues in Dutch politics in recent decades. From time to time the scrutiny of ethics even crosses national borders. In the 1970's, the American presence in Vietnam sparked great controversy in the Netherlands. Shortly thereafter people became increasingly critical of apartheid in South Africa and poverty in Third World countries. When it comes to these kinds of issues, Dutch people sometimes act as if they are morally superior to others, much to the dismay of those whom they target.

Members of the royal family are no exception to the moral obligation felt by Dutch citizens. Queen Juliana (who reigned 1948–1980) was known for her pacifism and social involvement. She once said in an interview that had she not been a queen, she would have been a social worker. Her four daughters are cast in the same mold. Rather than lead a jetsetting life in high society, Queen Beatrix spends much of her time studying social and cultural issues. Her husband, Prince Claus, devotes his week to the problems of developing countries. One of the Queen's sisters, Irene, is active in social work, world peace activities, and the women's movement. She has written a book in which she interviews women who have immigrated to Holland about their struggle for equal treatment in their new homeland.

Hundreds of thousands of Dutch people volunteer to assist people, animals, and the environment by joining associations and foundations. Charity drives are also extremely successful. Millions of dollars are donated annually to disaster victims or to children in undeveloped countries. Combining these private donations with the considerable sums granted by the Dutch government to Third World countries makes Holland rank second in the world among those countries providing nonmilitary developmental aid.

Deviance and Tolerance

Ask a group of North Americans how they would typify the Netherlands and someone will undoubtedly mention that it is a tolerant country, someone else perhaps adding that it might even be too tolerant. There is a good chance that these people have heard that Holland is a refuge for hard drug users. In actuality, these reports often center on just one district in Amsterdam. The red-light district, as it is called, has traditionally been a center for legalized prostitution. Though the business transacted there was different from that of the rest of Amsterdam, the district looked just like the rest of the city. The arrival of hard drug dealers in the 1970's changed the climate completely. In spite of sweeps by the police, dealers and users have turned it into an area where passersby feel unsafe. That district, however, is not representative of the whole country.

Prostitution has a long history in Holland, whose ports for centuries provided shore leave for sailors after long and lonely trips. Prostitutes have always been allowed to pursue their livelihood with relative freedom. According to modern law they and their bosses have the same rights and duties as other workers and employers. Prostitutes go for regular local government-sponsored medical checkups and are, if officially registered, entitled to receive allowances for holidays and illness.

But there are other reasons for the foreign view of Holland's tolerance. In big cities, for instance, soft drugs like hashish are sold openly in special shops. Soft-porn magazines can be found in any supermarket. Homosexuality and topless sunbathing are tolerated. Flipping through the national TV channels late at night, one may suddenly happen upon a striptease.

Here an obvious question arises: If the Dutch are so keen on uniformity and so wary of behavior that deviates from the norm, how are "aberrations" like these permitted? This is indeed a puzzling question, not in the least for the Dutch themselves. One part of the explanation is that the Dutch have always believed people should be allowed to be true to their own natures and convictions. Another part of the explanation is that the young adults of the 1960's and 1970's often accused people who preached "law and order" of a Fascist or Nazi mentality. This placed the authorities in the uncomfortable position of having to prove that they were different from Holland's former oppressors, something they could only do by moderating their plans or policies.

Whatever the causes, Dutch society is clearly experiencing a rapid transformation. Prior to the mid-1960's, deviant behavior was not tolerated. Established religious and political movements, each abiding by their own values and rules, were highly influential. An individual's behavior was expected to fit within the beliefs of the movement to which he or she belonged. Parents, police, ministers, and priests governed the behavior of their fellow citizens. Most people conformed or at least tried to make it appear so.

Twenty-five years later traces of that law-abiding period can still be found, but people have generally become less obedient and more critical minded. The influence people previously exerted over each other has diminished considerably. In Holland this development seems to have gone one step further than in neighboring Western countries. The once so neatly arranged Dutch society has exploded into a seemingly chaotic number of groups and subgroups, each defining its own life-style and norms to the extent society allows. The once-predominant traditional marriage has been replaced by a rich variety of relationships, all of which have the same legal status.

Roman Catholic and Protestant churches have dissolved into separate units, or base communities, as they are called. Members of these communities form congenial groups that meet in halls or in people's homes. Their meetings are of a more informal nature than the traditional church services. Priests and preachers are willing to discuss their religious and political views, and women have found an equal role in these communities. At the Vatican, Dutch Roman Catholics are known as the most rebellious members of the Church.

Adapting to Change

Holland, unlike several other European countries, has never taken a hard-line stance against change. On the contrary, newly acquired liberties originating in the large cities have now spread to the rest of the country. Some tough confrontations have taken place between the police on one side, students and squatters on the other. But these clashes have not produced permanent intolerance or drastic political solutions. Instead there is now greater sympathy for minority views. Many Dutch people now believe that choice of life-style is a private matter.

The old business sense of the Dutch resurfaces in this rather smooth adaptation to new developments. Netherlanders have learned that the world around them is changing constantly. Someone who wants to stay in business had better take a commonsense view of things and learn to adapt. Even if you personally disagree with the behavior of others, you may sometimes have to admit that the advantages of a truce far outweigh the advantages of harsh controls. If the gains outweigh the losses, you'd better be tolerant, even if you have to do it with a wry expression on your face.

In 1988 an American reporter accompanying an on-duty Amsterdam police team witnessed a stop-and-search operation in which a small amount of an illegal drug was discovered. Much to the reporter's surprise, a few minutes later the police gave the drug back to the man and let him go. When asked why they had done this, one policeman replied, "Suppose we take away his drugs and suppose we throw them in the river. He's most likely to go right back out and steal again to get money for more drugs. We're police. It's our task to prevent crimes. We may very well have just prevented one."

Another example of this attitude has arisen in response to bicycle theft. In 1986 more than 900,000 bicycles were stolen. In the big cities of western Holland, it is no longer a surprise if you return to find that your bike, left locked to a fence, has disappeared. People have given up all hope of solving this problem, and instead of investing money in a new bike, many young people simply resort to stealing another one themselves.

These examples typify the businesslike tolerance that has once again arisen in Holland. Something may be forbidden by law or principle, but in some cases a sober-minded weighing of cost and benefit may prove more effective. This does not mean that the Dutch always apply an "anything goes" approach. When what are viewed as serious crimes and offenses are involved, both the police and the judicial system take resolute action. The difference lies in a tendency to follow common sense rather than the official rules.

Pluralism and Freedom

Dutch tolerance is reflected in the country's law and politics. Holland was the first western European country to develop what is called a parliamentary democracy. Though originally little more than a carefully observed balance between competing provinces, this democracy has worked. In tolerating each other, the provinces kept their own hands free to carry on trade. In 1776 Americans searched for models for their proposed republic. James Madison, one of the authors of the U.S. Constitution, examined the Dutch system, and found it impracticable. The republic, he pronounced, is marked by "imbecility in the government, discord among the provinces, foreign influence and indignities, a precarious existence in peace, and peculiar calamities of war." But in Holland, the Dutch system led to the growth of a society in which some measure of freedom for all was assured. Political adversaries cooperated with each other because it was the only way to survive; citizens tolerated each other because it was the only way to do good business.

Holland's democratic system has withstood the test of time. Even to this day, political power is not held solely by the central government; provincial and local authorities, in addition to district water boards, exercise broad powers. Furthermore, no other country in western

High school students in Amsterdam.   Photo by Theo van Stegeren

Europe has more diverse spiritual and political movements and groups, and nowhere have these movements and groups established their own interests in the areas of education, broadcasting, trade unions, and leisure more thoroughly than in Holland. With new religious and political groups appearing every year, it appears that there is still room for more.

Obviously, Dutch tolerance is only a guarantee against conflict as long as no single group has a monopoly on power. So far, despite its shortcomings, the Dutch system has provided its citizens with a considerable degree of freedom for many centuries.

Preacher and Merchant

It has been said that two types have provided models for Dutch behavior: the preacher and the merchant. Both have long held central positions in the Netherlands. The merchant provided the money; the preacher provided the ideas. Their ways of thinking and living are still reflected in how the Dutch behave today. Diligence, temperance, and a responsibility to those who are suffering: These were the virtues the preacher imparted every Sunday from the pulpit. An examination of reality, a sober-minded tolerance, an international orientation: Those were the traits of the merchant. Together the two have left their mark on the identity of the Dutch people, perhaps explaining some of the paradoxes of the Dutch national character: a drive for conformity paired with a persistent tolerance; a moral, even moralistic, stance toward the rest of the world together with an emphasis on trade; a relentless orientation toward profit balanced by an insistent promotion of charity—all creating a climate of prosperity with little instinct for enjoying it.

Lately some people have expressed fears about the future of Dutch identity. In their eyes Dutch culture is already overloaded with foreign, and especially American, elements. How many more of these influences can the fragile culture of the Netherlands take? What will be left if a European union really does take shape in 1993? Will the preacher and the merchant be able to carry the Dutch into the future, or will one or the other be forfeited to keep up with a rapidly changing world? Only the coming decades will tell.

Land and Water

Land and water in Holland are like two sides of a coin. From an airplane the country resembles a quilt, patches of land interwoven with glistening patches of water. Closer up, cars, trains, boats, and bicycles can be seen crossing this patchwork. And all of it has been shaped by human hands. Forests have been replaced by houses, roads, and farmlands. Swamps have been filled in and rivers have been rerouted. Farmers especially have left their mark on the landscape, deforesting some regions and replanting others, digging up some places and refilling others.

The Netherlands is an area encompassing 13,967 square miles (36,165 square kilometers). (The state of Maryland covers an area of 10,577 square miles—27,383 square kilometers.) The size of the country is most easily expressed in terms of traveling time. The longest distance from the northernmost to the southernmost point can be covered by a car in less than four hours. Traveling east to west takes about three hours. Old well-preserved villages and towns, built in the sixteenth and seventeenth centuries, or even earlier, are scattered all over the country: Leiden, the town where the Pilgrims lived; growing cultural centers like Amsterdam and Maastricht; old trading towns like Veere, Middelburg, Gouda, Enkhuizen, Hoorn, Zutphen, and Deventer.

There is a variety of Dutch landscapes. The west and north are completely flat, so much so that the land outside the cities is simply called the *platteland* (flatland). On a clear day in the country, one can see miles and miles of meadows, farmland, and lakes. Panoramic views of the Dutch countryside, with scattered church towers and trees silhouetted against the sky, have been rendered by many Dutch painters.

Traveling to the east or south, one will see the landscape gradually becoming rougher and more sandy. Woods and moors appear. Old farms, sandy trails, and winding streams vary the scene. In the extreme southeast region, in the province of Limburg, Holland reaches its highest point. The word "high," however, is most misleading here. Dutch hills rarely exceed 600 feet (200 meters). The very tallest hill, Holland's highest elevation, reaches a height of 1,053 feet (321 meters). Dutch people often feel compelled to "climb" this Vaalserberg at least once in their lifetime. It is usually quite crowded there all year round.

Landscape Types

Holland may be small, but it is a country with a number of characteristic landscapes. Eight different types are distinguishable.

1. The Western *Polderland*　　The western part of Holland consists of lowland tracts reclaimed from beneath bodies of water. These

tracts, or *polders,* as they are called, lie completely below sea level. The dikes, canals, and ditches used to create *polders* in turn form the most visible features of this landscape. Peat, a fertile subsoil for pastureland, is most commonly found in this region. Meadow after meadow is covered with grazing cows, goats, and sheep, interspersed with thousands of nesting birds. People here typically reside in small villages or on remote farms dotted across the countryside.

2. The River Delta Region

The landscape in this part of the country is flat like the *polderland,* but the soil is made up of fertile river and sea clay similar to that which made up the entire region millions of years ago. Here, the Biesbosch National Park typifies the marshy areas that once made Holland an inaccessible and undesirable place to live. The southwestern islands are also a part of this region, an area long assaulted by storms and floods.

3. The Dunes

Holland is bordered along its entire coast by a strip of sandy hills or dunes. Varying in height from about 33 feet (10 meters) to 165 feet (50 meters), these hills are covered with various grasses and, in some places, pine forests. The dunes start from the delta islands and stretch along the west coast all the way to the islands north of the Friesland province. The *geest* (calcic) soil of the dunes is particularly suitable for growing tulips. Most parts of the dune region are open for recreational activities.

4. The Great Rivers

This region is characterized by the meandering rivers that crisscross its landscape and the towns and villages bordering the rivers. When the water level is high, these rivers, contained by hundreds of miles of dikes, rise above the surrounding landscape. Between the dikes and rivers are strips of fertile river forelands, called *uiterwaarden,* used during most of the year as fields or

The dune region forms an almost continuous barrier, with beach and sea on one side, land on the other. Grasses are planted to prevent sand from blowing away. The difference in height between sea and land is clearly visible.   Photo by Rijkswaterstaat

pastures. In the spring, however, when the rivers carry an overload of melted glacier water from mountains in France and Switzerland, these areas are easily flooded.

5. The High Netherlands

This landscape is found in the eastern and southern parts of the country. Holland's great rivers enter the country in this region and have cut deep lines, resembling valleys, in the earth. During the last ice age glaciers moved the earth in some places to form slopes and hills. Geologically speaking, the southernmost portion of Holland is the oldest, consisting of limestone and marl.

Farther to the north is an extensive sandy moor area, a high plateau without any major waterways. In another distinct area along the border with Germany, there are miles of straight canals, which were used to drain and reclaim a strip of what had once been impassable marshland.

6. The Veluwe   This landscape is one of a series of carefully protected natural reserves in the Netherlands. The Veluwe is a large grouping of hills, formed in the last Ice Age. There are woods, moors, and sandy plains. A part of the region has been set aside for the De Hoge Veluwe National Park, a wildlife preserve.

7. The North   The northern regions of the Groningen and Friesland provinces are as flat as the western *polderland.* Here, however, the soil consists of clay accumulated over many centuries. The area includes the Wadden Sea, an extensive region of tidal *wadden* (flats) that provides a unique wetlands wildlife area. The survival of this Wadden Sea is severely threatened by the pollution of the North Sea.

8. The Zuiderzee *Polderland*   The Zuiderzee (South Sea) was an inland sea until it was closed off by the Barrier Dam in 1932. Reclaimed between 1937 and 1967, land in this region is very new. Because rectangular plots are considered best for mechanized farming, the landscape is dominated by straight roads and canals. Much of this area was previously a part of the continent. Flooding in the thirteenth century had temporarily returned the land to the Zuiderzee.

Soil

Water and land in the Netherlands almost blend into a single, combined, terrain. The moisture level of Dutch soil is high. In the past, complete villages were known to vanish into the boggy ground. Houses today are built in a way that keeps this from happening. Many roads continue nevertheless to sink slowly under the weight of the sand, stone, and asphalt from which they are built. Every couple of years road builders are called in to reelevate highways. Some roads consist of ten layers of asphalt accumulated over the years.

In most countries, the composition of the soil dates back millions of years. Dutch soil, however, has changed profoundly over the last ten thousand years. The humid climate as well as the sea and rivers have buried considerable parts of the country under thick layers of peat—a soil type consisting primarily of carbonized plants. Older, more solid layers have disappeared far below the surface. Layers of peat and clay provide poor foundations and building houses is difficult. In Amsterdam, for example, builders run structural piles 66 feet (20 meters) into the ground to reach a firm layer of sand, providing only a partial

Village in South Limburg.   Photo from Cas Oorthuys archive

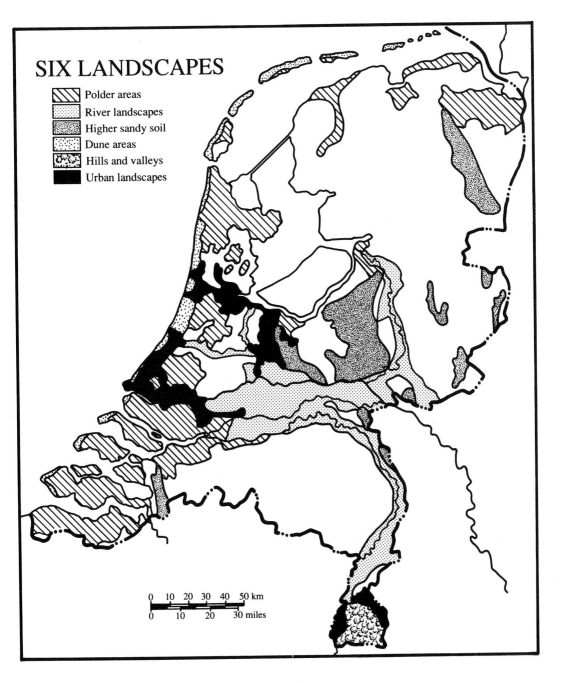

SIX LANDSCAPES

- Polder areas
- River landscapes
- Higher sandy soil
- Dune areas
- Hills and valleys
- Urban landscapes

0 10 20 30 40 50 km

0 10 20 30 miles

solution. A house can be built to stay level, but the soil around it will continue to sink. To counteract this, gardens and parks have to be raised at regular intervals.

Older soil can still be found in a few places in Holland, particularly in the middle and southern parts. The oldest visible piece of land in South Limburg contains sand and stone layers formed 300 million years ago. These older layers are still accessible, much to Holland's economic benefit. Modern mining technology can retrieve the four mineral resources stored in these layers: natural gas, oil, salt, and coal. In recent decades, natural gas has become an important and irreplaceable economic resource for Holland.

Flora and Fauna

Since the fourth century, when German tribes settled in the Low Countries, Dutch land has been parceled out to a variety of peoples. The more populous the country grew, the smaller the lots were cut. Nowadays the typical Dutch country landscape contains many rectangular parcels of land, separated by small channels, fences, and rows of trees. The greatest concentration of Holland's population is in the conurbation, or linked group of cities, called the Randstad Holland. The name "Randstad" literally means "city along the rim." Millions of people live within this long chain of large and moderate-sized towns located along the western coast. Important Randstad cities are Utrecht, Hilversum, Amsterdam, Haarlem, Leiden, The Hague, Delft, and Rotterdam. The towns are grouped around one "open" central region that has traditionally been called the "Green Heart" of Holland. The Green Heart is an area with lakes, meadows, canals, and villages, where many people go walking, biking, or sailing during the weekend. The area is now being threatened. New highways and railroad tracks are being built. What

The Provinces

The Netherlands is made up of twelve provinces. This is how the eight types of landscape, and the different kinds of soil, are distributed among the provinces:

Groningen	flat, clay and peat
Friesland	flat, meadows and lakes; clay
Drenthe	flat, moors and woods; sandy
Overijssel	flat, meadows and woods
Gelderland	gently sloping in the east; rivers; woods and moors; sandy
North Holland	flat, urbanized, dunes and beaches along coast, *polderland*; clay and peat
South Holland	flat, urbanized, dunes and beaches along coast, lakes, *polderland*; river and sea clay
Zeeland	flat islands and peninsulas, interconnected by dams, dunes, and beaches along coast; river and sea clay
Flevopolders	flat, *polderland*, straight roads and canals
Utrecht	half flat, half sloping, partly urbanized, rivers and woods
North Brabant	flat, woods, moors; partly sandy, partly clay soil
Limburg	flat, woods, peat and bogs in the north; hilly, marl soil in the south

were once villages are now being turned into suburbs, where many city dwellers hope to find better lives.

Scarce living space has made life difficult for Dutch wildlife. Long ago, animals like aurochs (large, long-horned oxen), bears, wolves, elks, and beavers freely roamed the Netherlands. By the eighteenth century, all had disappeared. The farther the people moved into the country, the more the animals retreated. Smaller species like the fox and the marten are the only two predators to have managed well. Two others, the badger and the otter, are in danger of becoming extinct.

Over the years, Holland's bird population has remained abundant. More than 150 bird species brood each year in Dutch pastural, Wadden Sea, and dune regions. In spring and autumn, millions of migratory birds make a temporary stop on their way to the north or south. Although numbers are high, birds in Holland are not completely safe. A national survey conducted in 1989 found that approximately fifty bird species are threatened with extinction. Encroaching agriculture and industry as well as diseases related to water and ground pollution are said to be the causes.

The story is even less optimistic for fish. Twenty of forty-six fish species are at present severely threatened or have already become extinct since the beginning of this century. Pollution is taking its toll, but the growing number of locks and sluices in the Netherlands is an additional problem, limiting the free circulation of fish through Dutch waters.

Dutch flora includes a great variety of trees, flowers, herbs, fungi, and moss. Oaks, beeches, chestnuts, birches, poplars, limes, pines, firs, elms, and willows are just a few of the tree species found throughout the country. The variety of plants is even more impressive, protected against advancing human civilization by the growing number of national parks.

Water and History

A perhaps apocryphal story circulating around Holland in the seventeenth century told of a cell in an Amsterdam prison that was specially equipped for the most hardened inmates. This cell, it seemed, could be flooded with water, which would gradually rise to the prisoner's knees, his waist, and eventually his lips. To survive, the prisoner was forced frantically to pump the water out with a hand pump within his reach. Many visitors to Holland mentioned the existence of the cell in their travel reports, which suggests that this horrible punishment was actually used. Netherlanders still use the expression "It's either pump or drown" (the Dutch version of "sink or swim") when someone's personal safety is at stake.

Whether the cell existed or not, the water punishment is an apt image of the history of the Netherlands. The Dutch have always struggled against the encroaching sea. The Latin motto on the emblem of the Zeeland (Sealand) province, written beneath a lion that fights to keep its head above the waves, reads: *Luctor et emergo* (I struggle and come up). The motto is an appeal for all Dutch people to help the country keep its head above water. The water punishment taught even the most wicked people that they, too, were part of the struggle to build and protect the nation.

Water has influenced the destiny of Holland in numerous ways. From prehistoric times through the nineteenth century, large parts of the country were nothing but swampland. Seeing little potential for agriculture or cattle breeding on the land as it was, early inhabitants began to fill the swamps, dig canals, and build dikes. Later when technology permitted it, pumps and windmills were used to regulate the water level.

To control the water effectively, farmers and citizens joined forces in governing councils called *waterschappen* (water boards). These councils discussed the plans and measures necessary to manage the water. Farmer or landowner, Protestant or Catholic, all were obligated to join in these efforts. If a storm was coming, differences and quarrels had to be quickly put aside. As the saying goes, these people were "all in the

Land and Water in Literature

The beauty of the Dutch landscape—its rivers, *polders*, and somber skies—has inspired the country's poets and writers for centuries. The lyrical poet Hendrik Marsman subtly interweaves the landscape and the water of the Netherlands in his poem "Thinking of Holland":

Thinking of Holland
I see broad rivers
languidly winding
through endless fen, lines of incredibly
tenuous poplars like giant plumes
on the polder's *rim;*
and sunk in tremendous
open expanses,
the farmsteads scattered
across the plain:
coppices, hamlets,
squat towers and churches
and elms composing
a rich domain.
Low leans the sky
and slowly the sun
in mist of mother
of pearl grows blurred,
and far and wide
the voice of the water,
of endless disaster,
is heard and feared.

Translated by James Brockway

Many prominent Dutch writers—among others Jan Slauerhoff, Simon Vestdijk, Martinus Nijhoff, Gerard Reve, Jan de Hartog, Nescio, Harry Mulisch—have used water as a theme in their novels. Some have embroidered on the saga of the Flying Dutchman, a legendary Dutch mariner condemned to sail the seas until Judgment Day. Others have used the theme to express the insignificance of humanity before nature and God. One of the finest novels on this theme is *The Waterman* (1933) by Arthur van Schendel. Set in the early nineteenth century, the book features Maarten Rossaert, a man who feels out of place in the hard-line Calvinist environment in which he lives. One day he breaks away from it all, taking his family and barge with him. Rossaert next joins a utopian religious community, the New Lights of Zwijndrecht, and uses his barge to provide financial support for the brethren. But there is no escaping fate. The water eventually takes the life of his mother, his sister, his son, and in the end, Rossaert himself.

The contemporary author Cees Nooteboom has written an original reflection on the Dutch and their landscape. The main character of his novel *In the Dutch Mountains* (1984), a Spanish engineer, says:

The Northern [Dutch] landscape, like the desert, suggests absolutism. Except that in this case the desert is green and filled with water. There are no enticements, roundnesses, curves. The land is flat, exposing the people, and this total visibility is reflected in their behaviour. Dutch people do not merely meet, they confront each other. They bore their luminous eyes into another person's and weigh his soul. There are no hiding places. Not even their homes can be described as such. They leave their curtains open and regard this as a virtue.

same boat." Out of sheer necessity, the Dutch learned to tolerate each other. They also learned to look at problems soberly instead of being swayed by strong emotions. Controlling one's own passions was vital to controlling nature.

Water is everywhere in Holland. The total length of navigable rivers and canals measures 3,020 miles (4,830 kilometers). The many branches of the Scheldt River in the southeast, and the Rhine and the Meuse rivers, intersecting the country at its middle, together meet the sea at the North Sea delta. The Rhine and Meuse have long acted as a natural border between the northern and southern regions of Holland. People on either side of the rivers refer to each other as "from above (or below) the great rivers."

Lakes can be found in most regions. Many Dutch cities and villages are built along canals and ditches. In one watery town called Giethoorn, canals and channels have taken the place of roads altogether. Millions of tourists come to see the locals embark in boats to do daily shopping or visit relatives. Giethoorn is not a typical Dutch town. Most Dutch people stick to the road to do their shopping. But there are numerous areas, especially pasturelands, where all traffic goes by boat. The peat on which these pastures rest "floats" on the water. Anyone who jumps up and down will feel the soil slowly surging under their feet.

Water as Enemy

The level of the water has always been more of a challenge to the Dutch than the actual quantity of water. Twenty-seven percent of the Netherlands lies below the normal level of the sea. The western provinces, where 60 percent of the population lives, lie entirely below sea level.

A permanent exhibit in the Amsterdam city hall illustrates the significance of water level for the Dutch. Three large glass tubes stand in the

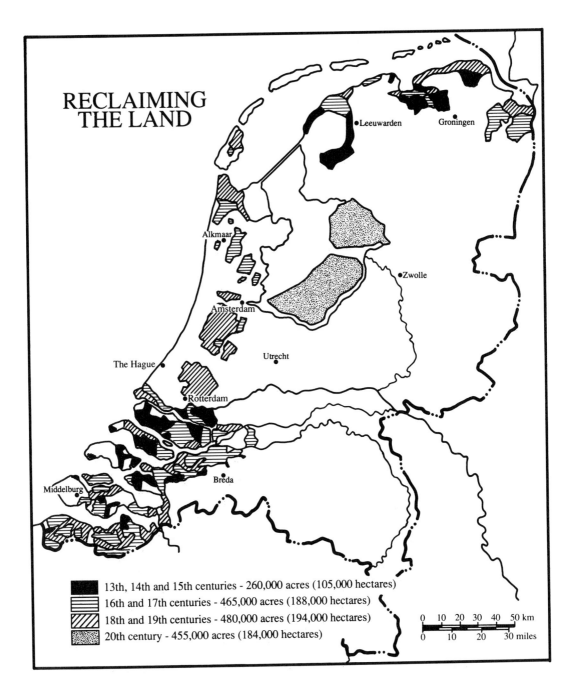

RECLAIMING
THE LAND

•Leeuwarden   Groningen•

Alkmaar

Amsterdam   •Zwolle

The Hague•   Utrecht•

•Rotterdam

Middelburg   Breda•

■ 13th, 14th and 15th centuries - 260,000 acres (105,000 hectares)
▤ 16th and 17th centuries - 465,000 acres (188,000 hectares)
▧ 18th and 19th centuries - 480,000 acres (194,000 hectares)
▒ 20th century - 455,000 acres (184,000 hectares)

0 10 20 30 40 50 km
0   10   20   30 miles

entryway, each filled with a blue liquid. Two tubes reflect the level of the sea near two coastal towns at that precise moment. The blue liquid rises or falls as the tide moves higher or lower. The liquid in the third tube stays at one constant level. It shows the height the sea reached during the flood of 1953, the most recent in Holland's history. In that year the sea rose to 14.75 feet (4.5 meters) above its normal level, breaching dikes and claiming many lives.

Throughout history, living in Holland has meant living dangerously. In winter and spring rivers that normally flowed peacefully through the flatlands suddenly rose and flooded their banks. Storms whipped up waves in the lakes, crumbling protective embankments. But the biggest danger came from the sea. With high tide the sea could swell up so uncontrollably that dunes, normally a natural barrier between sea and land, were swept away. Salt water invaded the land, cutting away new channels for rivers and creeks. Some of these have silted up; others are still intact today. Large areas of land were swamped forever, taken back by the sea. Off the Dutch coast lie quite a few medieval villages, buried forever at the bottom of the sea. Still visible is a series of islands, once belonging to the mainland but also torn away by the sea.

People living in the northern provinces of Groningen and Friesland began the process of building more durable protections against the sea. Between the first and thirteenth centuries churches or even entire villages were constructed on *terpen* (artificially raised hills). Many of these *terp* villages still exist. In the west, today the most populous part of the Netherlands, colonization took place slowly. By A.D. 1000 no more than 30,000 inhabitants, primarily Frisians, occupied the western coastal region. The name "Holland" originated here. One part of this coastal region, enclosed by dikes and covered with swampy wood and

Flood control dam on the Rhine River. Photo by Rijkswaterstaat

undergrowth, was called *houtland* (woodland), *holtland*, and, eventually, *holland.*

Despite centuries of labor and ingenuity, most protective devices proved insufficient. The sea still rose over the dunes and dikes. In 1421 the legendary St. Elisabeth's Flood (every medieval flood was named after a saint) swept away vast parts of southwest Holland. A modern reminder of that flood is the Biesbosch National Park. This swamplike, inaccessible piece of land was created during the St. Elisabeth's Flood and preserves the look of early Holland. This great flood also gave birth to a legend, still recalled today, about a child adrift in its cradle. A cat perched on the cradle kept it from capsizing. The site where child and cat washed ashore, alive and well, is still known as Kinderdijk (Child's Dike).

The Dutch have occasionally turned water into a deadly weapon. In the sixteenth century, breached dikes were used to deter the invading Spanish forces. The Dutch chose to flood entire regions, inundating fields with water and preventing further movement by the Spanish troops. The Spaniards were completely caught by surprise and forced to retreat.

During World War II, the Germans followed this example. By flooding one agricultural region after another—amounting to 7 percent of Holland's land area—the Germans were able to cut off the food supply of the larger cities. In the winter of 1944–1945 a serious famine broke out resulting in thousands of deaths.

Water has determined where people could settle in Holland. River intersections, river deltas on the seacoast, and bays providing shelter

The marks on the wall of a farmhouse in Alblasserwaard, in the province South Holland, show how high the water rose during floods in 1740, 1809, and 1819. Photo by Theo van Stegeren

from the open sea were all ideal locations for trading posts and shipping ports. Small towns emerged at these locations beginning in the eleventh century. These towns, soon to become cities, developed their own culture independent of the farmers living in the surrounding countryside. By the year 1600, this urban culture had become the dominant way of living and thinking in Holland.

Some towns were literally founded on the Dutch attempt to control the water. Dams were built on many rivers and streams to keep seawater from penetrating the land. These dams not only functioned as water barriers, but also prevented the passage of ships. Necessity gave birth to a new kind of business: unloading ships' cargoes arriving from sea and transporting them to smaller ships waiting on the other side of the dam. Villages bloomed into cities, called *damsteden* (dam cities) at these transit points. Amsterdam, Rotterdam, Edam, Volendam, and Monnikendam are the best-known *damsteden.* These cities furnished food and shelter for sailors, fishermen, and traders waiting for their next cargo.

Land Reclamation

The Dutch have not always been the victim of the sea's fury. Although they have often been forced to surrender land to the sea, sooner or later they have been able to force the water back and to reclaim much of this land. Taking all gains and losses into account, the balance remains slightly positive in Holland's favor.

Land reclamation goes back many years in the history of the Netherlands. Around the year A.D. 1000, coastal inhabitants began surrounding lowlands, where tides could freely enter and retreat, with dikes. The dikes were made up of sand, carried into place with shovels. To prevent the sand from being blown away, grass was planted on top of the dikes.

Construction of these walls was an effective protection against flooding. At the same time it prevented soil depletion caused by salinization. Keeping out the salty seawater made the soil more productive. Eventually these areas became dry and fertile enough to be used as pasture or farmland. Land reclamation in inland areas was also developed in the same period. Monks and farmers started to fill in marshlands, making them fit for building and living.

As techniques improved over time, people began to undertake more daring reclamation projects. The invention and improvement of the windmill—between the thirteenth and fifteenth centuries—made it easier to reclaim pieces of land from the sea. Superfluous water could be pumped away with the help of wind energy—an energy source readily available in Holland.

In the seventeenth century, urban investors saw the creation of new

Turning Water Into Land

In the late Middle Ages reclaiming land involved a number of steps. First a canal was dug around the watery or marshy area to be reclaimed. Next, rows of windmills were installed to pump the water out of the area into the canal. The surrounding land itself was generally below sea level and protected by dikes as well. Water pumped from the field could not simply be discharged into the sea. Instead, a complex system of waterways was used to carry this water up, step by step, to the level of the sea. This system, in which water travels through "staircases" to different water levels, is still the basis of the nation's water management system.

land as an excellent way to make money. Investment in the reclamation business skyrocketed. Investors' reclamation plans, highly ambitious for that time, were realized one after another. Numerous lakes were turned into *polders* and thousands of acres of new farmland were developed. These *polders* are still used today. The seventeenth-century villages in these regions are reminders of this period in Dutch history.

Zuiderzee and Barrier Dam

In 1886 a young engineer named Cornelis Lely was asked to explore the possibility of shutting off the entire Zuiderzee from the North Sea and of reclaiming huge areas of land within the enclosed area. Together with his technical staff, the thirty-two-year-old Lely produced seven detailed papers outlining a bold new approach to the problem. His plans mapped out three objectives: the reclamation of 556,000 acres (225,000 hectares) of new farmland within five great *polders*; the reduction of the coastline by 190 miles (300 kilometers); the provision of a 3,120-square-mile (8,112-square-kilometer) freshwater reservoir to be used for agriculture and industry as well as a check against saltwater infiltration into the subsoil.

With his report under consideration, Lely was appointed Minister of Transport and Water Affairs in 1891. He had hoped this would speed up the realization of his plans, but parliament continued to discuss and deliberate for years on end. Finally in 1918, during Lely's third term as Minister, a special bill was passed that provided funds for the construction of the Afsluitdijk (Barrier Dam), and the reclamation of four *polders*. A recent flood had demonstrated the vital importance of Lely's plan.

The construction of the longest dam ever built in Holland began in 1922 and took nine years. Builders worked day and night. The first shift started at five in the morning; the last shift worked until eleven at night under giant floodlights. The workers built the seaward side of the dike with mats of woven willow boughs, covered with clay and brick and topped with heavy basalt rocks imported and cut to a standard shape. In 1931 the last remaining channel was closed, a fleet of 231 dredgers, tugboats, floating pontoons, and other vessels supplying the necessary support and materials. The genius behind the project, Cornelis Lely, was not able to witness this historic occasion. He had died two years before.

The North Sea was now held back by one endless, beautiful Barrier Dam. The 217-mile (350-kilometer) coastline of the Zuiderzee, previously vulnerable to the North Sea's attacks, was reduced to a mere 19.8 miles (32 kilometers). With the North Sea cut off, only rivers and streams flowing from the interior of Holland were feeding the Zuiderzee, eventually transforming the lake's composition from salt water to fresh water. Moreover, the provinces of North Holland and Friesland were now linked by a breathtaking drive across the dam, with the North Sea on one side and a newly created lake on the other. After making this trip, the American historian Barbara Tuchman said: "To drive across [the Barrier Dam] with the sullen ocean on one side and new land on the other implies that at least for a moment one entertains hope for mankind."

In the years that followed, the lake was reclaimed step-by-step in accordance with Lely's plan. Successive reclamations converted the bottom of the old Zuiderzee into new land: the Noordoostpolder, 124 square miles (322 square kilometers); Oostelijk Flevoland, 140 square miles (364 square kilometers); and Zuidelijk Flevoland, 112 square miles (291 square kilometers). Today these vast *polders* reach as far as the eye can see, with stretches of fertile farmland intersected only by the geometrical roads and canals.

The flood of 1953 in Zeeland.   Photo by Rijkswaterstaat

The Deltaplan

"Disastrous Flood Engulfs Holland"; "Gale-swept Sea Breaches Dutch Dikes"; "Raging Waters Wreck 7 Centuries of Labor." These grim headlines in the American newspapers of February 1, 1953, were recorded by Gilbert M. Grosvenor and Charles Neave in a story in the September 1954 *National Geographic.* The story continued: "The two of us, juniors and roommates at Yale University, read on in horror. Last night, while we slept in the safety of our campus room, the tiny Netherlands, admired and loved by generations of Americans, had met with disaster at the hand of its ancient foe, the sea."

The night of February 1, 1953, showed that the closing of the Zuiderzee had not put an end to Holland's struggle with the sea. The country was hit by a devastating storm. The seawater quickly rose until, one after another, dikes as high as two-story buildings collapsed. Salt water gushed onto the countryside through 67 large and 495 smaller breaches in the dikes, inundating huge sections of southwest Holland. Many adults and children drowned immediately. Others climbed the roofs of their houses, waiting there for help. But with roads flooded and telephone cables down, rescue workers could not move quickly to save them. The flood claimed 1,835 lives and destroyed the homes of another 72,000 people.

New defenses against the sea were needed at once. Action could no longer be delayed. One year later the government introduced a plan that had been under deliberation for years. The Deltaplan, as it was called, outlined the construction of an unparalleled system of dams, dikes, locks, and bridges. Safety was an obvious concern, but the plan had other benefits as well. Large portions of southwest Holland, the primary market gardening region of the country, had filled up with salt from the sea. Sealing off the main inlets would halt that process and save the flower and vegetable industry. New freshwater reservoirs for public and industrial use and the creation of direct connections between the islands of Zeeland and South Holland were additional benefits.

The plan also turned out to have one serious disadvantage. One of the inlets affected by the plan, the Oosterschelde, was a unique ecological area rich in aquatic plants, birds, fish, mussels, and oysters. Daily tides supplied vital food for these plants and animals. Sealing off the inlet and eliminating the tides would disrupt the Oosterschelde's delicate ecological balance. Civilians and specialists cooperated to form action groups to exert pressure on the Dutch parliament to modify the plan. In the end their efforts met with success.

In 1976 a decision was reached to construct a special kind of dam

Construction of piers for the Oosterschelde Dam. Each pier is approximately equal to the height of a twelve-story apartment building. Once finished, piers were towed one after another to the planned site of the dam.   Photo by Rijkswaterstaat

that would not only protect the countryside, but would also preserve the ecosystem of the Oosterschelde. Hydraulic engineers came up with an ingenious, if costly, solution. A five-mile-long (eight-kilometer) dam would be constructed, equipped with a series of enormous sliding doors that could be opened and closed automatically. Under normal conditions these doors would be left open, allowing tides to flow in and out freely, but they could also be lowered during a storm tide. The dam was officially opened in 1985. As planned, the system preserved the precious natural environment. The Oosterschelde Dam alone ultimately

cost the Netherlands 8 billion guilders (more than 4 billion dollars), exceeding total costs for the remainder of the Deltaplan.

On the national level, complete water management is entrusted to a special department called the Rijkswaterstaat (National Water Affairs). With its billion-dollar budget and highly specialized know-how, this department resembles a state within a state. Rijkswaterstaat engineers are not just in charge of day-to-day water management. To a large extent they develop the plans that determine Holland's use of the limited space it has.

Recently the Rijkswaterstaat has been faced with a new challenge. The threat of rising global temperatures, perhaps caused by the "greenhouse effect," poses serious problems for the global water management system. Leading geologists estimate the sea level will rise an additional 3.3 feet (1 meter) over the next century. Melting glaciers and polar ice caps are one cause, but because warm water occupies a larger volume of space than cold water, rising seawater temperatures raise the sea level even higher.

In Holland, plans have been developed to adapt the country's coastal fortifications to that new challenge. Waterways will have to be restructured, sand dunes will require reinforcement, and sources of drinking water will have to be protected against penetrating seawater. Seen in the long term, a rise in sea level of 2.6 feet would require an investment of up to 10 billion dollars.

Present-day Holland is much safer than the Holland of a half century ago, but the Dutch have learned that there is no end to the struggle against the sea.

A First Impression

It's still dark on the Dutch *platteland*, but boys and girls assemble outside their village. When everybody has arrived, they jump on their bikes and set out for a long trip to school. They ride single file, the oldest ones in front where the wind is at its strongest. Every day they make their strenuous ride over dead-straight bikeways, the flat fields and meadows to their left and right.

Little seems to have changed in this daily ritual over the last fifty years. The bikes, the wind, the meadows—all the symbols of traditional Dutch life are still there. But behind the scenes rural life in Holland has been transformed. Few of these boys and girls still dream of taking over their parents' farms. Many farms that lined the road twenty years ago have been closed or rebuilt into luxury homes; only those that have

A contest for skutsjes, *large, flat-bottomed sailing boats, in the northern province of Friesland.* Photo by ANP

been computerized and converted to function like factories survive. Older brothers and sisters find jobs or begin university studies elsewhere and turn their backs on their hometowns.

Today only 5 percent of the Dutch population lives in areas with under 5,000 inhabitants. Nearly two thirds of the population lives in towns with between 10,000 and 100,000 inhabitants.

The Morning

Daily life in the cities and suburbs of Holland starts between seven and eight o'clock to the buzz of electric alarm clocks and radios. Central heating or gas heaters warm up houses in the early hours. People get ready for the day with news on the radio forecasting a day of changeable weather and listing the many traffic jams throughout the country. Half an hour later, the Dutch gather around their breakfast tables. These are not necessarily traditional families. More than 40 percent of Dutch people live alone or with friends. There is a growing number of people who choose to live alone because they have not met Mr. or Ms. Right or who simply prefer to preserve their independence.

The Dutch usually eat bread for breakfast, preferably whole wheat bread, freshly baked at the bakery around the corner, spread with margarine or butter, followed by marmalade, cheese, peanut butter, chocolate sprinkles, or colored sprinkles. For lunch, marmalade and peanut butter are replaced by cold cuts and more cheese. Tea, coffee, and milk are the common breakfast drinks. Many children prefer cereal to bread, served with milk or often yogurt on top.

Family at breakfast table.   Photo by ANP

The Weather: Changeable

The Netherlands is said to have a mild marine climate, the average temperature in January being 35° F (1.7° C), and in July, 63° F (17° C). Average annual rainfall exceeds 29.58 inches (740 millimeters), spread fairly evenly throughout the year. But Holland's climate is actually completely unpredictable. Winters are usually cold but can sometimes be mild; summers are mostly warm but can be rather cool as well. Winter is usually cold enough to bring some snow, but not enough to freeze over Dutch waterways. When there is ice, however, most Dutch people are quick to don their skates for an outing on the channels, lakes, and canals.

In the summer months, from June to August, there will be a few fairly hot days. On exceptionally hot days, when temperatures can rise above 77° F (25° C), schools are closed due to the "heat wave." On hot summer weekends, beaches, parks, and terraces are filled with scantily dressed sun worshipers. But when a fresh gale blows in, the heat can disappear quickly. Dutch weather can be quite unpredictable even in a single day. Heavy rainfall in the morning can be followed by a sunny afternoon. People are accustomed to

On weekdays Dutch breakfast is fast and easy. Despite the Dutch television networks' attempts to promote morning programs, television is rarely watched in these early hours. Most people simply have no time for it. A short conversation, a glance at the newspaper, and everyone's gone. Ways of getting to work vary. One worker leaves home at seven in the morning. Five sandwiches, a plastic bottle with milk, and an apple taking a raincoat along "just in case." On average it rains 120 days a year in Holland. The wind, coming from all directions across the flat land, practically never ceases blowing. Holland gets only 3 or 4 days a year on which there is no wind at all.

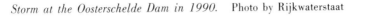

Storm at the Oosterschelde Dam in 1990.   Photo by Rijkwaterstaat

are safely held under carrier straps on his bicycle. After his arrival at work he and his colleagues have a short chat about last night's TV shows and then get to work. His wife, who works farther from home, takes the car. She gets stuck along with the millions of commuters who create miles of traffic jams every day. The city streets and highways are filled with aggressive drivers, puzzled pedestrians, loaded buses and streetcars. Cyclists race amidst all this commotion, neglecting as many traffic rules as they can. Thousands of commuters arrive late at work, just as they did the day before.

At School

After breakfast all children between five and sixteen years old, the age range for compulsory education, leave for school. Millions of students, most of them on foot or on bicycle, take to the streets. Kindergartners are taken to school in special baby seats mounted on the handlebars of their mothers' or fathers' bicycles. Some parents even carry two or three of these little passengers on their bikes, one in front, one or two in back.

Most schools are housed in modern buildings. Classrooms have large windows, looking out on the schoolyard or the street. Practically all the schools in Holland belong to a nationwide system of public schools. Except for a small minority of more exclusive schools, school fees are equally low everywhere. Most schools are tax supported, which keeps fees low. In general schools are attended by children from all levels of society.

Dutch schools offer flexible "route systems." Students have the opportunity to switch from one "track" to another. A girl, for example, might discover at the age of fourteen that she prefers vocational rather than an academic education. She can then change to another type of school, usually within the same community of schools. Students from a lower social class often start out on the bottom rung of the school ladder. If teachers and parents discover that a child can do better, they

There are approximately 10 million bicycles in Holland. Riding a bicycle is not restricted to any one class in society. Rich and poor alike use this mode of transportation for shopping, going to work, or just spending free time. Photo by Theo van Stegeren

can stimulate him or her to move upward to a school with better academic facilities.

Through such openness and flexibility, schools in Holland have contributed considerably to the blurring of distinctions between rich and poor that dominated Dutch society in the past. Simultaneously, however, schools continue to reflect society's divisions, even if not in the rigid ways encountered two generations ago. A child of an unskilled worker enters the school system with different expectations than the child of an executive. An unwritten law, even in the Dutch educational system, is that children of unskilled workers and immigrants have lesser chances of becoming professionals than children from more affluent homes.

In Holland, the choice between inexpensive and expensive schools is not a "hot issue" as in other countries. The choice is instead defined along other, typically Dutch, lines: Although practically all schools are publically supported, they have different views on religion and philosophy of life.

At present primary and secondary schools are evenly split among the three main religious views: One third are nonreligious, one third Protestant, and one third Roman Catholic. A small number of Islamic schools has recently joined the ranks. Parents are well represented on the boards of parochial schools, empowered with protecting the particular identity of the school. Their freedom of action is more limited than it was in the first half of the century, however: Nowadays all schools in the Netherlands provide essentially the same curriculum and prepare their pupils for the same final exams. Differences are usually found in the selection of teachers. Parochial-school teachers approach subjects like politics, ethics, and sexuality differently than their nonsectarian equivalents, and perhaps add religious lessons. Some orthodox schools keep homosexual teachers out of their schools. Freedom of education, in their opinion, means they may "protect" their pupils against "bad influences." Others see this as a violation of the constitution, which explicitly defines discrimination "on any basis" as unlawful.

Although differences among the schools may seem small, they still prove to be decisive for most parents. Three out of four Dutch people believe the choice between a religious and a public education for their children is crucial. That is precisely why so many children take long bike trips to get to their schools: Their own villages may not have the schools of the right religious persuasions.

At Home

While men, boys, and girls are on their way to work and school, adult Dutch women are harder to find in this rush-hour traffic. Most Dutch women are housewives and remain at home. Of women between twenty-five and forty-nine years old, one third are employed outside the home, far fewer than in most other European countries. Among women with children, the percentage of working women is even lower. Of all mothers with children under six years old, only 27 percent are employed. (In the United States, by comparison, 57 percent of this same group works.) The fact that most women stay at home is partly due to the relatively high unemployment rate in Holland. But even in periods of practically full employment, women's participation in the labor market has remained low compared to other countries. The Dutch love their domestic life, and women remain the center of the family. The women's movement—otherwise very successful in Holland—has not been able to change this tradition in Dutch society. Men are still wary of changing their roles. Few take the burden of full-time care for children and the household on their shoulders. The creation of more part-time jobs and a network of day-care centers could change this thinking. Unfortunately, most employers are slow to create part-time jobs and often fail to provide day care for their employees' children.

At Home in Holland and America

Although a comparison between middle-class Dutch and American home life is hard to make—life in Rotterdam and New York may be more similar than life in Alaska and Santa Fe—some general differences stand out. Whereas American boys and girls have many opportunities to escape from their family's company—by watching their own TV set, for instance, or by driving their own car—Dutch children grow up surrounded by family members. Voluntarily or out of necessity they engage in collective activities throughout the day. Family members usually have breakfast, lunch, and dinner together, they drink coffee, talk about school, wash the dishes, use the same car, have arguments.

Though Americans may spend more time out on their own, Dutch girls and boys generally enjoy more freedom of expression than their American counterparts. "If you visit a Dutch family," an

On the other hand, few women demand a radical reversal of roles. The traditional feeling that mothers are responsible for bringing up their children is still widespread. Many women want to be there when their children come home from school, just as their own mothers did. Fathers often remain aloof from the daily upbringing of their children. The division of roles between mother and father is reflected in this quotation from Herman van Veen, one of Holland's most talented entertainers. As he remembers it: "When it was time for my two sisters and me to come home from school, my mother would always be standing in the doorway waiting for us. Then we'd get tea and zwieback." During the day his mother arranged everything in and around the house; his

American observed, "abandon all hope of being able to hold a reasonable conversation." Loud-mouthed children place themselves chattering and dancing between host(ess) and guest, cuddle up to Mother, stroke her face and hair, or wriggle around in her lap, "continuously asking stupid and unnecessary questions."

Dutch children are often treated as responsible persons. If they, for example, are supposed to be silent, the phrase "that's not allowed" is endlessly repeated in all variations before harsher measures are applied. Many parents will even try to explain to them why it is necessary to be silent, instead of simply forcing them to do so. The hope of the educators is, of course, that children will really learn to behave if they see why they should. Dutch children are allowed, often encouraged, "to be true to themselves." They learn to define themselves in terms of *who they are*, rather than in terms of *what they have.* For them personal virtues and happiness are at least as important as careers and money.

father would come home later. When he had gotten into mischief, however, his mother would often say, "You wait until your father gets home," leaving the final word to her husband.

Dutch housewives usually take care of daily grocery shopping. Men who wish to do their share of the shopping are hard put to find the time. Practically all shops in Holland close at six P.M. and remain closed till the next morning. On a normal weekday, one can shop only during working hours. The only exception is in the larger cities, where stores may stay open until nine in the evening once a week. But in general, weekday shopping remains almost exclusively the responsibility of the woman of the house.

Large retail chains and consumers' organizations repeatedly pressure parliament to extend shopping hours, but the owners of small shops refuse to go along with such a change. They fear that if retail chains are permitted to extend their shopping hours, competition will become more intense than it already is. Numerous political debates have focused on the issue, but the Christian parties and the trade unions have been able to keep the laws as they stand. Shopkeepers and their assistants, they maintain, are entitled to the same regular home life as other workers. Dutch tolerance is at a loss here. Public opinion is highly divided over whether shopkeepers are a threatened minority that desperately needs governmental protection or just a stubborn minority imposing its will on the rest of society.

Food and Celebration

Holland sits down to dinner between six and seven in the evening. With the wide variety of Dutch households, it is difficult for anyone to make firm statements about *the* Dutch kitchen. As in North America, supermarkets now offer food specially packaged in smaller portions for the millions of people living alone.

The growing presence of people from foreign cultures, with their own traditions, tastes, and life-styles, makes it hard to keep up with the changes in Dutch dinner style. Until the late 1960's, the picture was clear. Dutch meals were comprised invariably of potatoes, vegetables, and meat. Every day had its "special": On Mondays, for instance, most people had meatballs for dinner; Friday was fish day. Desserts were not served. But with the new prosperity, traditional eating habits "exploded" in all directions. The Dutch, not particularly chauvinistic about their own food, welcomed hundreds of exotic dishes to their cuisine. An average weekly menu nowadays may include salade niçoise (French), spaghetti bolognese (Italian), spare ribs (American), nasi goreng (Indonesian), moussaka (Greek), and pea soup (Dutch). Other ethnic groups have introduced their own specialties as well. Restaurants, shops, and markets offer Surinamese, Turkish, Moroccan, Chinese, Israeli, and Spanish food.

Dutch Traditions

Traditional Dutch food is usually served in the wintertime. People then tend to fall back on delicious though perhaps less refined dishes like *hutspot* (hodgepodge), a stew of potatoes, carrots, and onions, served with slices of fried pork. Other popular Dutch meals are *zuurkool* (sauerkraut) and *boerenkool* (kale), both served with sausage. Herring is a popular snack in Holland. Herring stands are found on many street corners and bridges. Regular customers drop by once or twice a week and eat raw herring on the spot. Eating herring requires a special technique: You take the fish at the tail, lift it above your tilted-back head, and then start eating, lowering it slowly into your mouth.

For most Dutch, the daily routine follows a strict timetable. Breakfast, coffee break, lunch, teatime, dinner—there is a fixed time for every one of these rituals. The end of the working day sets in abruptly after six o'clock. At dinnertime, the streets are practically empty. Here and there someone rushes off to a team practice or a meeting of an action group or association, but in general the streets are pretty desolate. Yet a stroll through these empty streets can be very instructive. The Dutch prefer not to close their windows with curtains or shutters, enabling passersby to quickly steal a glance at the domestic life going on inside. Although looking inside is considered impolite, one who is bold enough to ignore that rule will learn a lot about Dutch life. The first thing one notices is the variety of plants and even small trees on the windowsills. In an effort to make the home more livable and personal, nature is brought indoors, often accompanied by crochet and all kinds of baubles.

The Immigrants and Their Children

Holland is a multiethnic society. Turks, Moroccans, Surinamese, Antilleans, Spaniards, and Italians are just a few of the new ethnic groups that color the traditionally white Dutch society. Apart from the fact that they or their parents were not born in the Netherlands, these various groups do not have much in common. Mediterraneans and North Africans immigrated to Holland in the 1960's and early 1970's. During those years Western European countries recruited and employed migrant workers to relieve their labor shortages. Many North Africans have had problems with the Dutch language. At the same time their Islamic faith often conflicts with the dominant patterns of Dutch society. Moroccan and Turkish parents, for instance, find it hard to accept the freedom their children enjoy. Some of them are used to choosing husbands for their daughters, a custom difficult to maintain in a modern Western society. Moroccan boys often rebel against their fathers' control. Many drop out of school and turn to drugs and crime.

Ethnic minorities on market day.   Photo by Theo van Stegeren

This cartoon criticizes Dutch people who maintain that there is no racial problem in Holland, ignoring the fact that they themselves have strong negative feelings about immigrants and nonwhite people. "They aren't dangerous," the man says complacently about his two dogs, named Racism and Xenophobia (hatred of foreigners). Illustration by Peter van Straaten

People from the former Dutch colonies of Surinam, Indonesia, and the Antillean islands have immigrated to Holland in distinct "waves." As their home countries gained independence, these immigrants decided to move out for political or economic reasons. Most of them are now Dutch citizens and speak Dutch fluently.

Only 4 percent of Holland's population belong to nonwhite ethnic groups, a low percentage compared to Belgium's 9 percent or France's 7 percent. But locally the proportions are different. Half of the immigrant population lives in four of Holland's big cities, comprising 19 percent of Amsterdam's population and 15 percent of Rotterdam's. Racism and discrimination manifest themselves in various, often subtle, forms. White people, for instance, sometimes avoid sitting next to black passengers in a bus, make racist jokes, or refuse jobs to blacks. The position of ethnic minorities on the labor market is vulnerable; immigrants are overrepresented among the unemployed.

A Typical Home

Behind this natural screen one may find people watching television (present in every household) or video (in one out of every two households). Prime-time game shows are particularly popular in Holland. People at home enjoy knowing the right answer in a quiz before the contestant does. They laugh about difficult tasks contestants have to accomplish, like crossing a canal with the use of a pole or crawling through mud as quickly as possible. Others are reading, playing games, or just passing a *gezellige* (cozy and intimate) evening with relatives and friends. Children have their own rooms, where they do their homework or listen to music.

With increasing prosperity, more and more people pursue their *gezelligheid* outdoors. In the morning hours women like to drink their coffee in one of the many coffee shops. The coffee shops look a bit like home, but there is a variety of types of coffee. These coffee shops are not only for housewives. Students come by, and businesspeople take their lunch there. Most coffee shops close at six o'clock, but around that time the cafés, which also serve liquor, are already open. These cafés—in Amsterdam alone there are some 1,000 of them—have the intimate atmosphere of people's living rooms: Tablecloths cover the tables, paintings or posters hang on the walls, and flowers stand in vases. The cafés open their doors during the afternoon and stay open until twelve or one o'clock at night during the week, during the weekends until two or four o'clock. Every group of people—workers, soccer fans, students, Hell's Angels, young Christians, Rastas, punkers, and squatters—has its own café, where they play their own kind of music. There are dance cafés, billiard cafés, eating cafés, soft-drug cafés, and also low-life cafés.

Throughout the year, there are occasions when family life is at its best. The Sinterklaasfeest (Saint Nicholas's Feast) is one such, very Dutch, occasion.

The Celebration of Sinterklaasfeest

On the eve of the fifth of December, the Dutch celebrate the birthday of Sinterklaas (Saint Nicholas), which officially falls on December 6. Sinterklaas is an old, white-bearded man in a red suit who delivers presents to good children. Sinterklaas arrives from Spain, where he lives, several weeks before his birthday. From that day forward, children anxiously await his gifts. The saint, as parents explain, rides at night over the rooftops on a white horse along with his helper, Black Pete. Good children are rewarded with presents. Naughty children may receive no present at all—or, worse, they may be punished. Black Pete, who always carries a rod with him, may give them a spanking or even put them in a gunnysack and take them back to Spain. Every night children place one shoe in front of the fireplace in the hope that Sinterklaas and Pete will drop presents down the chimney. The next morning children run to see if there's a present in their shoe. When they're lucky they'll find goodies—chocolate, marzipan, or Dutch candy like *speculaas* (a type of spiced cookie) and *pepernoten* (spicy nuts)—placed there secretly by their parents.

On the eve of the fifth, the Dutch give gifts to each other, children believing and adults pretending that these have been delivered by Sinterklaas. Gifts are opened one by one in the family circle, each accompanied by a poem to be read aloud by the receiver before the present is opened. Usually the poem teasingly criticizes the receiver of the gift for some bad habit. Occasionally, discussion arises about the racial implications surrounding Black Pete. Should a black man be portrayed as someone to be afraid of? Most people, however, consider this to be nonoffensive and refuse to abolish the age-old tradition.

The Sinterklaas feast has a long tradition. Saint Nicholas actually lived from A.D. 271 to December 6, 342 or 343. He was the bishop of Myra, a city in Asia Minor. Over time devotion to the saint has extended to all parts of the world. Some historians assume Sinterklaas's riding over the rooftops on a white horse is a pagan heritage: In the centuries before Christianity, tribes in Holland believed that Wodan, a powerful god with a long gray beard, rode his horse across the skies.

In the seventeenth century Dutch Protestant settlers in New Amsterdam (now the city of New York) replaced Nicholas with the friendly, white-bearded figure who became known as Santa Claus.

Celebration of Koninginnedag.   Photo by Theo van Stegeren

A special national holiday is the Queen's birthday, called *Koningin-nedag*. On that day every town has parades, sports events, and fairs with merry-go-rounds, whirligigs, dodg'ems, ghost trains, and gambling machines. In more traditional towns citizens hold official meetings and sing the national anthem in honor of the Queen. In the bigger cities *Koninginnedag* has become a massive cultural happening, at which the national anthem is no longer heard. Here the Queen's birthday is not the central theme of the day; it is just used as a welcome occasion to engage in a spontaneous, carnivallike celebration. Beginning early in the morning, sidewalks are covered with people selling secondhand clothes and all kinds of knickknacks. Hundreds of pop and jazz bands play live music in the streets or on boats in the canals. People eat and drink until late in the evening.

On most evenings the streets are peaceful and quiet. Life returns to the streets only briefly around eleven o'clock. Then scores of people leave their homes once more to take their dogs for walks around the block. No laughing matter in a country where it rains so often.

Early History

In 1976 prehistoric tools were discovered in sandpits near the Dutch town of Rhenen. The news plunged Dutch archaeologists into a heated search for artifacts from what had previously been a little-known historical period. Amateurs from across the country also raced to Rhenen to begin digging. Thousands of tools were found, varying from simple round stones to carefully carved implements called celts, which were believed to have been used by people roaming the Low Countries almost 150,000 years ago. These findings indicate that the earliest Netherlanders lived by hunting large animals like the wood elephant (similar to a rhinoceros), the hippopotamus, and the red deer. These gatherers of berries, nuts, and fruits probably survived right up to the dawning of the last Ice Age. Then cold northwestern winds began to blow, covering the Low Countries with drifted sand. As the cold increased, the area

A terp *in the province of Groningen. In the early days people sought refuge on the mound during high tide.*   Photo from Cas Oorthuys archive

turned into a frozen flatland for what was to be an immensely long period of time. Human life disappeared completely.

Only in about 14,000 B.C. did people gradually return to the Netherlands. The first to enter the country were herders from the east seeking plains to graze their reindeer. As the climate gradually became more hospitable, the sea level fell and larger areas of land were uncovered. Hunters and cultivators then chose to stay in the Low Countries on a more permanent basis.

Time Line

57–51 B.C.	The Roman military commander Caesar incorporates the Low Countries up to the Rhine River into the Roman Empire
ca. A.D. *400*	Romans retreat from Low Countries; Franks, Frisians, and Saxons settle
734	Franks defeat Frisians; large sections of Low Countries under Frankish rule
843	Treaty of Verdun, the first of a series of treaties in which the Carolingian Empire is divided
1363–1482	Burgundian period
1500	King Charles V of Spain inherits the Hapsburg Netherlands
1555	King Philip II succeeds Charles V; his attempts to restore order in the Netherlands provoke resistance
1568–1648	Eighty Years War between Netherlands and Spain
1576	Pacification of Ghent: the southern and northern provinces agree to resist the politics of Philip II
1579	Union of Utrecht
1584	William of Orange assassinated
1585	Taking of Antwerp; refugees flee to Amsterdam
1588	Republic of the Seven United Netherlands

Early Mediterranean peoples made their way slowly across Europe, leaving behind remnants of their housing, agriculture, and weaponry. Archaeological evidence indicates that all the routes taken to northwestern Europe passed through the Low Countries. In turn, the region

1648	Treaty of Munster; republic recognized as independent state
1652–1654	First,
1665–1657	Second,
1672–1674	Third,
1780–1784	and Fourth Anglo-Dutch Wars
1813	Fall of Napoleon; Holland becomes a monarchy
1815	Kingdom of the Netherlands officially founded
1830	Belgian Revolution
1839	Belgian independence recognized by the Netherlands
1848	New Dutch constitution
1914–1918	First World War—the Netherlands stays neutral
1940–1945	Second World War—the Netherlands occupied by Germany
1949	Indonesia recognized as independent republic
1958	European Economic Community founded
1962	New Guinea under the authority of the United Nations
1963	New Guinea brought under the administration of Indonesia
1975	Independence of Surinam

functioned as a meeting ground where diverse cultures interacted and influenced each other. In later centuries the Netherlanders would derive their economic strength from continuing to fill this role.

The Romans

The expansion of Roman armies into Europe in the first century B.C. provided the Netherlanders with a more ominous form of contact with Mediterranean people. The Low Countries, however, were located in too remote a corner of the continent to be quickly conquered by the Romans. Only in 57 B.C. did the first Roman explorers enter the Dutch region. For the Romans, life in the Low Countries seemed very inhospitable. In contrast to their own temperate homeland, they found only a low-lying, marshy plain in a cold, wet climate. The country seemed barren of potential farming land and mineral resources. The population was also hostile. In the northernmost reaches of the country, the Romans encountered the Frisians. These were the people who had established *terpen* to protect themselves against the sea. Twice each day, with the coming and going of the tide, the sea flowed in and flooded all but the artificial hills upon which the Frisian people lived. One Roman historian visiting the region could not quite tell whether these people belonged to the land or the sea: "During the flood the inhabitants look like sailors, but come low tide, they look like shipwrecked victims."

Realizing that the Low Countries were strategically important, the Roman commander Julius Caesar set out to conquer the region, but met with only limited success. At the cost of many lives the Romans were finally able to take over most of the country, except in the north where the Frisians managed to hold their ground.

The Romans remained in the south late into the fourth century A.D.

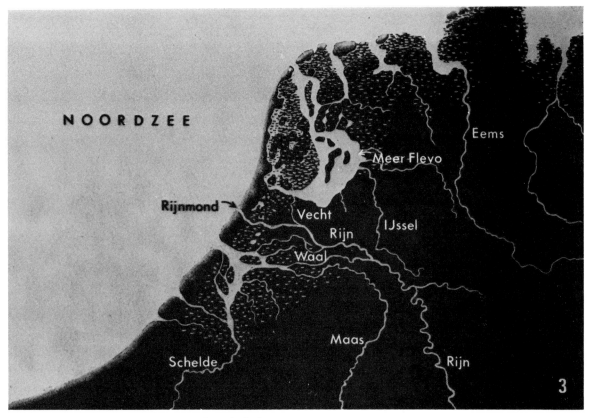

The Netherlands as it must have looked 2000 years ago. FIBO Zeist

Charlemagne

Around A.D. 400 the Netherlands entered a new period. Gradually new tribes, mostly Franks and Saxons, migrated into the Low Countries from both the east and the south. These people settled in the most habitable areas and from there began cultivating the land. Pathways were cut through the woods, watery areas were drained, and farmland was eventually created. Little is known about these tribes, but there is no doubt that the settlers are the direct ancestors of today's Netherlanders. They are also the people who gave the Dutch landscape the look that would in part be preserved into the twentieth century. Villages in the eastern

The Dutch Language

The nucleus of the Dutch culture is its language. Or to put it more strongly: Without its language, the Netherlands would lose its national identity altogether. Many foreigners don't know that Dutch is an independent language, probably misled by resemblances among Dutch, English, and German. But Dutch grammar and vocabulary make up a unique language, spoken daily by the 15 million inhabitants of Holland. In addition, the language is used by 6 million inhabitants of northern Belgium, whose version of Dutch is usually called Flemish. One of the official languages of South Africa, called Afrikaans, is a derivative of Dutch. Speakers of Dutch and Afrikaans are able to converse with relative ease.

Today, the Dutch language contains an extremely rich variety of words. Dutch and Belgian linguists have worked for more than a century on a comprehensive dictionary, called the *Woordenboek der Nederlandse Taal* (*Lexicon of the Dutch Language*), usually abbreviated to *WNT*. This dictionary brings together all words that belong or have belonged to the written Dutch vocabulary. The first volume of the *WNT* was published in 1864, and since then, its authors have reached words beginning with the letter "V." Currently numbering 36,500 pages, the *WNT* is, even in its present unfinished state, the bulkiest dictionary in the world.

Dutch left its mark on many other languages, particularly in the sixteenth and seventeenth centuries, when the Dutch established trading posts on every continent. American words like "yankee," "dollar," "golf," "skates," "sloop," and "skipper" are derived from Dutch.

The following table shows some resemblances among four languages historically related to each other: English, German, Frisian, and Dutch. All four belong to the West Germanic language group, and, in turn, to the Indo-European language family. Frisian is spoken by an estimated 500,000 people, living mainly in the province of Friesland itself. Frisian is their mother language, although Dutch is also spoken. The Frisian language has its own grammar and vocabulary and is incomprehensible to people from outside the region. When Frisian is spoken on national television, subtitles are used.

ENGLISH	FRISIAN	DUTCH	HIGH GERMAN
year	jier	jaar	Jahr
chaff	tsjeff	kaf	Kaff
goose	goes	gans	Gans
us	ús	ons	uns
sweet	swiet	zoet	süss
four	fjouwer	vier	vier
church	tsjerke	kerk	Kirche
ear	ear	oor	Ohr
seek	siikje	zoeken	suchen
day	dei	dag	Tag

Frisian is remarkably similar to English. No other foreign language is closer to English than Frisian. This kinship can be traced back to the early Middle Ages, when early versions of both languages were spoken in the North Sea region. English and Frisian have words in common that are very different in Dutch—for example:

ENGLISH	FRISIAN	DUTCH
boy	boi	jongen
key	kaei	sleutel
yet	jit	toch

part of the Netherlands are reminiscent of this period not only in name but also in the pattern in which they were built.

The Dutch language itself originates in this period. The Franks, who steadily moved northward, used Romance—that is, Latin-based—dialects, while the Angles, Saxons, and Frisians spoke Germanic languages. Over the centuries that followed, the different languages spoken by these people fused into one tongue. The language barrier between the Romance and Germanic dialects, originally located in the north of present-day France, moved northward and came to rest straight across present-day Belgium. There it still is today: The south of Belgium is French speaking; the north speaks Flemish, a variant of Dutch.

Model showing German tribes entering the Low Countries over the Rhine River. Photo by FIBO Zeist

The Low Countries were roughly divided into territories. While the Angles and some Saxon tribes moved on to England, other Saxons settled in the eastern part and the Frisians in the northern and western parts of the Low Countries. The Franks settled in the south and from there expanded their territory. In two military campaigns (in 689 and 734) they defeated Frisians and Saxons and gained control over most of present-day Holland. The Frankish kings—devout Christians—considered it their holy task to eradicate pagan ideas and customs like cremation, the belief in nature gods, and the use of black magic. On their behalf preachers spread over the country to convert the population to Christianity. One of them, later canonized, was Willibrord. This missionary was once sent to the Frisians. There he used the water of a sacred pagan well to baptize a convert. The Frisians, so the story goes, flew into a rage. Their well was desecrated, and they demanded a human sacrifice to appease their gods. Willibrord and his helpers were forced to play dice for their lives. The one who lost was buried in the beach sand up to his neck (a common punishment in this coastal region) and then left to await the rising tide.

In 768 all power over the Frankish Empire, later called the Carolingian Empire, was taken firmly into the hands of a new King, Charlemagne. The empire by that time encompassed a large portion of western and central Europe. The rule of Charlemagne brought a period of relative peace and cultural revival to the Low Countries. The issue of religion, however, remained an ongoing source of conflict. Charlemagne envisioned the Christian religion as the moral foundation for his empire. He sent messengers to the Low Countries who proclaimed in every village square that men or women who refused to be baptized or who continued practicing pagan customs would be put to death. The Frisians and Saxons initially ignored the campaign, but decades of preaching and conquest eventually converted all of them, those resisting having been banished or put to death.

Romanesque church in Maastricht, Limburg.   Photo by VVV Maastricht

In 800 Charlemagne was crowned Emperor by the Pope in Rome. He saw himself as successor to the Roman rulers of the past. But, just like those emperors nine hundred years before, he could not exert full control either over Europe in general or in the Low Countries in particular. In the Netherlands Charlemagne had to delegate his power partly to local dukes (in Brabant and Gelderland), counts (in Holland, Zeeland, and Flanders), a bishop (in Utrecht), and various barons. Instead of obeying Charlemagne's rules, these men tried to gain more power for themselves. After Charlemagne's death (in 814) the empire crumbled further. The Low Countries were the same as they had always been: a collection of regional, autonomous territories.

In 843 the Low Countries were inherited by one of Charlemagne's grandsons, Lothaire I. The King gave the control of this land over to local nobles and clergy. Over time these local rulers gained an iron grip upon their territories. (Nominally, however, the Netherlands were still part of the Holy Roman Empire.) A long feudal period (1100–1400) began, in which peasants and their families were the serfs of nobility and clergy. They were expected to farm the land, transport commodities, build barns, and do hundreds of other chores for their masters. In addition, a fixed part of the wheat, pigs, and cheese they produced was for their masters. The serfs received no money for their labor and products, only protection. The serf women were at the disposal of the master. Some serfs escaped and tried to live as free peasants where their masters could not find them, but it was risky. Anyone who was caught had his tongue pulled out and his ears cut off.

Many noblemen consolidated their authority with harsh punishments and military violence. The power of the church was of a different kind. Children were often forced by their parents to enter monasteries or convents but were sometimes not able to endure the isolation. One of the earliest Dutch medieval poems (1374) tells of Beatrijs, a young woman in a convent who has fallen in love with a man from the outside world. *"Minne worpt mi onder voet"* (literally, "love throws me under its foot," meaning "love has defeated me"), she confesses in a prayer to the Virgin Mary. She abandons her nun's habit and the keys of the convent at the foot of Mary's statue and flees to meet her lover. For seven years they lead a happy life until one day Beatrijs finds that he has deserted her. To support herself and her two children she is forced to live as a prostitute for seven more years. Remorseful, she returns to the convent to discover that Mary has stood in for her. Her absence has never been noticed.

The poem, well known in its time, highlighted the central importance of religion in the life and thinking of the people. Only by returning to the convent could Beatrijs regain happiness. But the poem also demonstrates that people devoted to religious life were sometimes deeply confused by feelings that conflicted with their faith.

The Burgundian Empire

In the fourteenth century the power of the nobility in the Low Countries declined. Its economic monopoly was undermined by the rise of trading towns. While the nobility's wealth came from control of land and farming, the towns developed a new kind of economy, in which money was the key to success. The main towns in Overijssel and Gelderland were part of the German Hanseatic League, a chain of cities united as trading partners to compete with other mercantile cities. The Dutch Hanseatic towns such as Kampen, Deventer, Zwolle, Harderwijk, and Zutphen were located along the inland shipping routes between the Baltic Sea and Flanders. They served as ideal transfer points for trading wheat, wood, animals, ceramics, and all kinds of food and clothing.

Merchants and nobles came into conflict in many places. No single town or regional sovereign, however, was strong enough to conquer the entire area. This offered the Burgundian Empire—already covering large parts of present-day France—the chance to bring several northern and southern provinces under its rule. During this Burgundian period— from 1363 to 1482—the southern provinces (now the Flanders region of Belgium) achieved an economic strength that soon surpassed the power of the Hanseatic League in the north. Initially relying on a flourishing textile industry, Flanders quickly developed into the economic heart of Europe. In the magnificent cities of Bruges, Antwerp, Ghent, and Malines (Mechlin), streets and markets were crowded with merchants of all nationalities. Burgundian court life in Brussels (now the capital of Belgium) was renowned for its opulence, the place where many famous Dutch artists, including the painter Hieronymus Bosch (1450–1516), were to find their inspiration. This period has clearly left its mark on the culture of Belgium and the southern provinces of Holland. While people in the north tend to be austere, the inhabitants of this area are still known for a more loose and lavish way of living, often referred to as a "Burgundian life-style."

Despite the central power of the Burgundian ruler and despite economic cooperation among several provinces, real political unity was still not possible. None of the individual provinces were prepared to give up their autonomy. No name like "the Netherlands" or "Holland" was used to identify the region, although the term Landen der Verenigde Nederlanden (Countries of the United Netherlands) was used on official documents. There was no common language. Members of the nobility spoke French. Latin was spoken at the universities. On the streets and markets a mixture of dialects and languages could be heard. The modern eastern provinces of Friesland, Overijssel, and Gelderland were still regarded as part of Germany.

In spite of their great accomplishments, world history was to have no

The Gothic Style

During the Gothic era (thirteenth and fourteenth centuries) Dutch workers began to unite together in guilds to defend their rights. These guilds were associations of people who practiced the same trade or craft. There were guilds, for instance, of carpenters, bakers, spinners, and painters. New guild members had to go through a set series of learning stages before they were allowed to call themselves "masters." Standards of craftsmanship and quality were maintained by the guilds.

The artistic guilds, where religion was a powerful source of inspiration, helped the arts flourish for the first time in many centuries. Architecture, painting, and sculpture in this period reflected changes in the rest of society. Romanesque architecture (flourishing from 1050 to 1200) considered worshipers as humble, God-fearing creatures, seeking shelter from the almighty presence of the Supreme Being. Church windows were accordingly kept small or omitted completely.

But with the advent of the Gothic period, master builders and artisans took a different approach. The introduction of great windows in church walls reflected the opening of people's minds. People began to reach out for God. They felt confident enough to look upward, to turn to the light. Churches and other buildings were no longer constructed primarily along horizontals, as they had

great role in store for the Hanseatic towns or the Flemish cities. That place was reserved for the western provinces of Zeeland and particularly Holland. Diversity was the strength behind these provinces' economies.

been in the Romanesque period. Now they were characterized by a predominant verticality. The most visible feature of this change was the pointed arch.

Gothic St. Jan's cathedral in Den Bosch, North Brabant.   Photo by E. van Mackelenbergh

Holland's fertile soil allowed intensive cattle breeding and flower and vegetable growing, while productive industry and artisanship developed in the cities. The biggest boom was in the fishing industry. Herring, commercially the most lucrative fish, moved in great numbers from the Baltic to the North Sea around 1500, signaling golden times ahead for the Dutch fishing companies. An effective way to strip the herring of its gills and entrails was invented, improving its taste and making it easier to preserve. Larger fishing nets were developed, and a new type of fishing ship was constructed that far surpassed competing ships in speed and capacity. Some 1,000 of these ships—*haringbuys*, as they were called—were in operation at the beginning of the sixteenth century.

For the Dutch, one trading deal triggered another. Fishers extended their activities to other kinds of fish and soon took over Europe's international fishing trade. Trade had likewise developed with countries such as Spain and Portugal in the south, where salt, indispensable for the storage of herring, was readily available. The Baltic region was another big customer for herring fishers. Soon a trade network blossomed that featured not only herring, but also wood and wheat.

With the development of the *fluyt,* a new type of cargo ship, the Dutch lowered transport costs. The fluyt sailed with only six to twelve crew members, half that required on foreign ships.

Church Reformation

By 1477 various marriages among ruling European families placed the southern, Burgundian, Netherlands under the control of the royal Hapsburg family. The Hapsburgs dreamed of making Flanders a prosperous and strategic post within their own empire, which was an extension of the Holy Roman Empire. Their enormous territory was governed by a branch of the family living in Madrid. Spain at this time was an old-style feudal country, where—in contrast with sentiment in the Netherlands—those in authority expected blind obedience. The Hapsburgs were also devout members of the Roman Catholic Church, which did not enhance their popularity in the Netherlands, where the revolutionary ideas of the German monk Martin Luther had just begun to take root. Luther had translated the Bible into everyday language and had openly protested against what he considered to be the abuses of power by the Church of Rome.

The Reformation movement, split up into different sects, quickly gained momentum in the Netherlands. In the eyes of these reformers the Roman Catholic Church was tied with the rule of the Hapsburgs. Local groups began secretly to organize their own religious meetings. People came from far and wide to hear these preachers speak while armed sympathizers guarded against any interference. The most powerful of the Reformation groups, the Calvinists, did not recognize the Pope's authority and rejected the worship of saints and many of the rituals practiced by the Roman Catholics. The Calvinists believed any church layperson—farmer, needlewoman, fisherman, or merchant—was capable of understanding the Bible without the intervention and guidance of priests or ministers. Dutch families would spend an entire Sunday discussing matters such as the kind of life-style that could guarantee someone a place in heaven.

William of Orange

Sooner or later the Dutch were bound to collide with the Holy Roman Empire of the Hapsburgs. When in 1555 the new Spanish King, Philip II, ascended the throne, he immediately took steps to restore discipline in the Netherlands by introducing a national system of taxation and harshening the punishment of Dutch Protestants. He installed a special tribunal that arrested every Protestant who dared to cast a critical glance at a holy picture. The tribunal—the Dutch called it the Blood Council— pronounced more than 9,000 judgments. Thousands of people were put on the rack and 1,150 people were sentenced to death. Although the

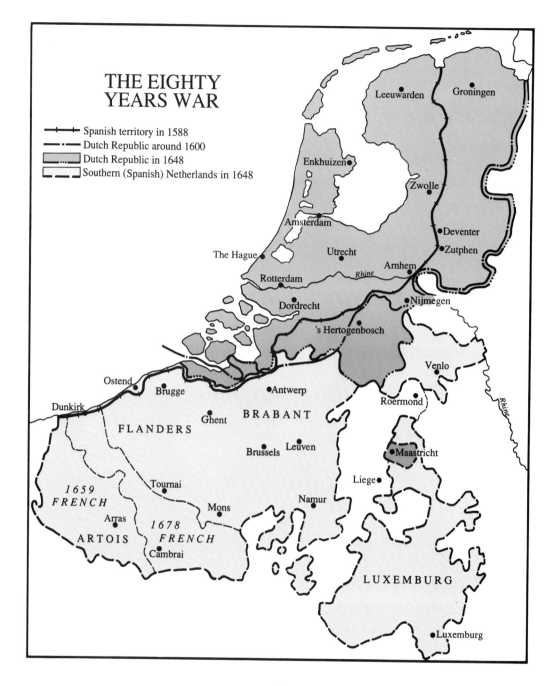

THE EIGHTY
YEARS WAR

Spanish territory in 1588
Dutch Republic around 1600
Dutch Republic in 1648
Southern (Spanish) Netherlands in 1648

Leeuwarden
Groningen

Enkhuizen

Zwolle

Amsterdam

Deventer
Zutphen

The Hague
Utrecht
Arnhem

Rotterdam
Rhine

Dordrecht
Nijmegen

's Hertogenbosch

Venlo

Ostend
Brugge
Antwerp
Roermond

Dunkirk
Ghent
BRABANT
Rhine

FLANDERS
Maastricht

Brussels
Leuven

Liege

1659
FRENCH
Tournai

Mons
Namur

Arras
1678
FRENCH

ARTOIS
Cambrai

LUXEMBURG

Luxemburg

judgments were harsh, convicted Protestants kept on testifying to their faith, even on their way to the gallows or stake. The Spanish judges thereupon prevented this by piercing each victim's tongue with a glowing awl. The imperial family, however, could not successfully impose these measures from so far away. On the contrary, the Spanish reign of terror and the Roman Catholic inquisition eventually united the Dutch provinces as allies. By 1568 a religious and political confrontation was no longer avoidable. War (which came to be known as the Eighty Years War) broke out between the Netherlands and Spain. As the war grew fiercer, more and more citizens, guided by the belief that no human being—not even the Spanish King—had the right to demand absolute obedience from another human being, became involved in the resistance.

Politically the provinces were in a complicated position. In the first place, not all of the seventeen provinces joined the revolt against the Spanish King. Several southern provinces chose the side of the Spanish, meaning that the revolt became a civil war. In the second place, the northern provinces were not able to organize their resistance. At the onset of the war, a supreme governmental body called the States General was established, which included representatives from each of the provinces. Unfortunately, in the States General a unanimous vote was needed to make any decision. Since no province wanted to be forced to do something against its will, the national government remained hopelessly ineffective.

A Fleet on Land

Coordination was eventually achieved under the command of William of Orange. This nobleman, ironically one of the provincial deputies appointed by the Spanish King, organized a fresh wave of attacks against the Spanish enemy. William, and the Dutch, had their finest hour in the relief of Leiden (1574). Leiden had been under siege by the Spanish army since 1573. Every counterattack had failed, and the population was starving. Persuaded by the arguments of William of Orange, the local authorities decided to try the only remaining solution: They ordered the dikes around Leiden cut. At the same time they asked their allies to sail a fleet with Dutch rebels over the inundated fields toward their town. The strategy seemed to work. A fleet of flat-bottomed barges, crewed with thousands of rebels, sailed over the flooded fields from Delft toward Leiden. But then the barges got stuck at a road where the water was only six inches deep. The people in Leiden, growing more desperate daily, started eating dried animal skins and leaves from the trees. The mayor, confronted with an increasingly mutinous population, said that the townspeople should kill him and eat his body rather than surrender to the enemy. Then, on September 29, a heavy storm combined with high tide raised the water level. The barges floated off and caught the Spaniards totally by surprise. On the night of October 3 the people of Leiden saw the cold and wet Spanish troops, carrying torches to light the way, wade away from the city. One boy had the courage to leave town and take a look in the enemy's entrenchments. He discovered they were empty. The next day the famished population celebrated its liberation by eating white bread, fresh herring, and *hutspot* they had found in the camp of the Spaniards. To this day the people of Leiden celebrate October 3 by eating white bread, herring, and *hutspot*.

William of Orange felt encouraged by the outcome of the conflict in Leiden. In 1576 he successfully united the seventeen northern and southern provinces at a meeting in the city hall of the Flemish town of Ghent. But the freedom of religion this agreement, called the Pacification of Ghent, provided for met with resistance from both Protestants and Catholics. When the southern provinces were subsequently reconquered by the Spaniards, seven northern provinces united in a new defense treaty, the so-called Union of Utrecht (1579). This Union is of great historical significance, as it formed the foundation for the later state of the Netherlands and set the boundary between territories that would later become two separate countries: the Netherlands and Belgium.

Alarmed by the sudden unity among his enemies, King Philip II proclaimed William an outlaw and offered a reward for his murder. In 1584 Philip's edict had the desired effect: William of Orange was shot dead at his home. It was a heavy blow for the Dutch resistance.

Antwerp Falls: A Republic Is Born

One year later a Spanish attack hit the southern provinces hard. The city of Antwerp was taken in 1585. Thousands of merchants, artisans, preachers, scientists, and artists fled to the north to the free province of Holland. Most were Protestants fearing the loss of religious freedom under the Roman Catholic Spaniards. This massive immigration brought new economic power to Dutch cities, importing precious knowledge, artistry, and business contacts. The northern provinces tried to paralyze economic life in Antwerp, Bruges, and Ghent, all in Spanish hands now, by blockading the Scheldt River and the coastline. The Flemish towns were isolated from the outside world. The northern provinces profited greatly from the situation as all shipping traffic was forced to use their ports.

On the battlefield the Netherlands were still not able to defeat the Spaniards decisively. The seven northern provinces—Holland, Zeeland, Utrecht, Gelderland, Overijssel, Friesland, and Groningen—realized that they could not afford to maintain their ineffective form of government much longer. They asked the King of France and, later, the Queen of England to rule over their country, but both refused. With no other possibility left, in 1588 they founded the Republic of the Seven United Netherlands. In practice this meant that the seven provinces intensified their regular meetings on military affairs. Real unity was still far away. The republic had no president, no parliament, and no political parties. Creating a common constitution was especially difficult, because the most powerful partners had the largest say in politics, threatening the rest. The *regenten* of Holland province—the wealthy members of the Dutch upper class who paid 58 percent of the republic's budget— tended to dominate the republic's affairs.

But if it did not solve all political problems, the new republic could at least wage its war against Spain more effectively. The northern provinces, now calling themselves the Republic of the Seven United Netherlands, possessed sufficient resources to form well-trained armies. Most of these armies were not Dutch and were instead made up of mercenaries from other European countries. In 1600 the army of Prince Maurice, William of Orange's son, included forty-three English, thirty-two French, twenty Scottish, eleven Welsh, and nine German companies. Only seventeen companies were Dutch.

Expansion Overseas

At the end of the sixteenth century, Holland stood on the brink of what would later be called its Golden Age. The towns of the provinces of Holland and Zeeland, particularly Middelburg, Veere, Hoorn, Enkhuizen, and Amsterdam assumed leading roles in shipping and trading. Worldwide sea transport was primarily a Dutch affair. Gigantic fleets, sometimes comprising more than five hundred ships, sailed every European sea. Even when commodities were not carried by Dutch-owned ships, they were carried by ships that had been built by the Dutch. At the very height of its power in 1670, the Dutch trading fleet, numbering some 10,000 ships, was three times larger than the English fleet, and bigger than the fleets of England, France, Portugal, Spain, and the Germanic nations combined.

Exploitation of trade in the Far East was exclusively consigned to one new company: the *Verenigde Oostindische Compagnie* (United East India Company). Though representing only a minor share of Dutch trade, the VOC's projects were spectacular. In 1636 the Dutch were the only outsiders permitted to establish a trading post in Japan. The Netherlands held this privilege for more than two hundred years.

The VOC reached the American continent in 1609. In a vain attempt to find a passageway to India, one of the company's ships, the *Halve Maen* (*Half Moon*), discovered what would later be named the Hudson River. The name comes from the ship's captain, Henry Hudson, an Englishman working for the Dutch. Following an unexpected confrontation with Native Americans, one crew member recorded the excitement of encountering another people: "We heard the screaming of human voices on the coast. We thought they were Christians who had been left behind and we sent a boat for them. But we soon discovered that these were savages, who seemed to be very glad of our arrival." One hundred twenty-five miles upstream, near the present city of Albany, the *Halve Maen* was unable to continue its exploration.

Back in Holland, Hudson and his crew reported their findings. The Dutch government saw the desirability of establishing a colony in America and tried to persuade its citizens to emigrate to the other side of the ocean. The campaign, however, was unsuccessful. Dutch traders who settled along the Hudson River wanted to do business, not develop a Dutch colony. Three decades later, ten thousand people were living on the shores of the Hudson and on Manhattan Island. Only five thousand were of Dutch origin.

Amsterdam, Center of the World

During most of the sixteenth and seventeenth centuries Amsterdam was the center of world trade. Anyone who wished to buy or sell commodities in bulk inevitably turned to Amsterdam. Here lived the merchants with the money and contacts to buy, stock, and resell wares to third parties around the world. Here were the banks with exchange facilities for all foreign currencies. Here were the insurance companies, the bank commissioners, and the brokers. In its Golden Age, the city of Amsterdam grew dramatically. Its population rose from 31,000 inhabitants in 1578 to 200,000 in 1660. The city's canals, arranged in concentric circles, were lined with spacious four-story homes and warehouses. A contemporary guide called the city "the warehouse of the world, the seat of opulence, the rendezvous of riches, and the darling of the gods."

The center of Amsterdam. The canals, dug in concentric circles, are bordered with ancient warehouses and mansions.   Photo by Dienst Ruimtelijke Ordening Amsterdam

Like other trade cities, Amsterdam acted as an independent state. Profit was often more important to its merchant leaders than the city's loyalty to the other provinces. Amsterdam actively supported the Spanish blockade of the port of Antwerp, and it maintained trade relations with Spain during its war against the Dutch republic. Preventing the revival of Antwerp was as important to Amsterdam as beating the Spanish, if not more so.

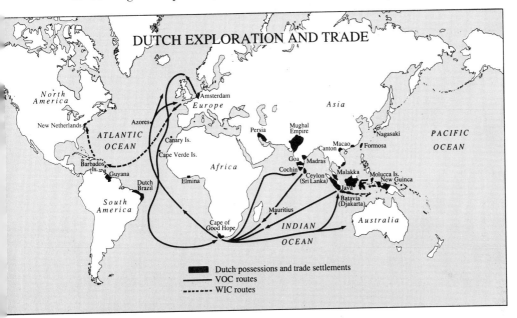

The headquarters of the trading companies VOC and the *Westindische Compagnie* (West Indies Company, known as WIC), were in Amsterdam. These companies were privately owned—shares were sold on the stock exchange of Amsterdam—but protected by the government. The VOC and WIC created a worldwide network of settlements and trading posts. One North American settlement was called New Amsterdam in New Netherlands. New Amsterdam was taken in 1664 by the British, who renamed it New York in honor of the King's brother, the Duke of York. Briefly recaptured by the Dutch in 1673, it was finally sold to the English in 1674. Holland received Surinam in return, an area in Latin America that cut its colonial ties with Holland in 1975.

Trade in the West

A second Dutch trading company, the WIC, was also involved in the founding of the New Netherlands. Founded in 1621, this company was granted a trading monopoly in the western hemisphere. Together with the VOC, the Dutch network could justifiably be called "worldwide." The WIC sailed primarily to the West Indies and Latin America. Profiting from the ongoing war between Spain and Holland, WIC ships captured many Spanish ships carrying cargo in the same region. In the bay of Havana, six large Spanish galleons loaded with silver tried to evade the Dutch fleet. The Dutch captain, Piet Heyn, eventually captured the ships and forced the Spanish to surrender. The entire silver fleet, which today would be worth 11 million guilders (nearly 6 million dollars), fell into Dutch hands without any further resistance.

Heyn himself felt the conquest had not matched the heroism of past undertakings. But back home Heyn and his crew were astonished by the fanfare of welcoming salutes, speeches, and patriotic hymns. One of these songs, with the refrain "He has won the silver fleet," is still sung by the Dutch to cheer on teams at sporting events.

Slavery

The slave trade was the WIC's main source of income. Willem Bosman was one of its most successful slave traders. As chief merchant he organized hundreds of slave shipments. He believed that blacks were diabolical: "All Negroes are, without exception, villainously shrewd, treacherous, and unreliable."

Ships for transporting slaves would leave Holland loaded with all kinds of commodities: textiles, weapons, alcohol, and ironwork. Upon arrival in West Africa, these commodities would in turn be exchanged

Tulip Mania

In 1636 and 1637 Holland was under the spell of the tulip. Everybody wanted to have one, and some people paid up to a thousand guilders (about five hundred dollars) for one bulb.

The mania for tulips arose around 1634, when it became fashionable—especially in the cities—to offer ladies expensive tulips. Having a bed of tulips in one's garden was a sign of wealth. Within one year the demand for tulips rose dramatically. So did the prices. Investing in tulips became profitable. During those years of war and looting, in which saving money had proved to be a hazardous business, investing in tulips seemed the perfect solution. Most of the time the bulbs were buried safely underground, where no plunderer would find them. But once planted, they grew quickly. Next summer's flowers could be sold while they were still under the ground.

Florists and flower traders began speculating. Tulips were resold several times before they had even come to bloom. Prices soared. Tulip lots could be traded for prices five, sometimes ten, times higher than their original value. The trade now began attracting more speculators who wanted to make a fortune quickly. Men and women, maids and farmers—nobody wanted to miss the boat. Tulips were exchanged for horses with carriages, cows, or paintings. The Dutch authorities had just begun considering introducing a special tax on the tulip trade when, in February 1637, the demand for tulips was suddenly over. The market collapsed. Some people had made a fortune; many—among them famous painters like Hals and Rembrandt—had lost all the money they had.

for captured Africans. From there the second part of the trip, or the "Middle Passage" as it was called, began. The slaves were branded and then crowded into the ship's hold without clothing. Under atrocious conditions—it was normal for 15 percent of the slaves to die during transport—the human "merchandise" was transported to North and South America. There the blacks were exchanged again, this time for sugar, tobacco, cotton, and coffee. These were then transported back to the home port.

The slave trade made Willem Bosman and many of his colleagues rich men. A slave delivered alive yielded two to three times the sum for which he or she had been purchased. So strong was the commercial appeal of slavery in Holland that the Dutch remained involved in the slave trade longer than most other countries. Slavery was not abolished in the Dutch colony of Surinam until 1861, two years before the Emancipation Proclamation in the United States.

CHAPTER V

The Golden Age

Modern Holland cannot be understood without looking back to the sixteenth and seventeenth centuries. Many of the virtues and vices regarded as typically Dutch took shape in this "Golden Age." Preachers and merchants molded Dutch character and promoted its moralism, tolerance, and sober, businesslike attitude. The ideas of the humanistic philosopher Erasmus and the legal theorist Huig de Groot had a permanent effect on Dutch thinking. Painters like Rembrandt and Vermeer made their lasting contributions to the artistic legacy of Holland. The Golden Age laid the economic base for present Dutch wealth. The modern cities of Rotterdam and Amsterdam both came to prosperity in this period.

What was Dutch life like in those days? Many foreign visitors praised

Holland for its freedom, simplicity, and fairness. Others felt that life in Holland lacked style and grandeur. One Spanish envoy was unable to believe his eyes when he saw members of Dutch parliament sitting down to a lunch of plain bread and cheese on a bench outdoors. Michiel de Ruyter, the highly respected admiral of the Dutch naval fleet, sometimes asked honored guests on board ship to excuse him while he went to feed his chickens.

The Dutch were never overly impressed by authority figures. The father of the house, whose control went undisputed in other countries, was challenged regularly in Holland. Wives exerted at least as much influence on family life as did their husbands—which is still true today. A prominent Italian visitor observed that Dutch women did all kinds of tasks assumed by men in other countries. They were managing pubs, keeping financial records, or working as salespeople. Several of Amsterdam's leading trading companies were managed by women. Dutch males frequently complained of this, half jokingly, half seriously. The most celebrated poet of the Golden Age, Joost van den Vondel, wrote: "One woman is too much for a thousand men."

For children, the absence of absolute authority also had its advantages. As many visitors observed with amazement, Dutch children enjoyed an unusual amount of freedom; on the other hand they did not always receive sufficient parental attention.

The Age of Erasmus

Relationships within the family mirrored the country's political relations at the time. While in surrounding countries kings, emperors, and popes exerted absolute power, the Netherlands did not have a strong central government. People clung to a way of life in which their own village or town, their own religion and their own traditions took priority

At the back of the house, a family is saying grace around a barrel that serves as a table for their simple meal. The painting reflects the Dutch belief in the sacredness of the family and the view that laypeople, rather than the church, were the center of religion. The sunflower (left) is a symbol of the family's piety. Attributed to Jan Steen, *Prayer Before the Meal*, 1667–1671. John G. Johnson Collection, Philadelphia

over feelings of nationalism and unity. For a very long time, the Eighty Years War was not conceived of as a war of independence. Nobody envisioned one united and independent Dutch state. The war was a series of conflicts in which various provinces and religious groups resisted Spanish taxes and tried to ensure tolerance and power for local authorities.

The Spirit of Freedom

The Dutch person's desire to be his or her own boss first manifested itself in the early Middle Ages. Life in the western provinces centered on *polder* reclamation. The draining of marshes was a heavy, unrewarding task. Landowners had to offer their peasantry all kinds of benefits. Laborers were granted pieces of land, which they could lease at a very modest rent or even sell to others. In comparison with rural workers in neighboring countries, these people were treated more as free citizens than as serfs or slaves.

Dutch geography played a vital role in the emergence of the country's spirit of liberty. With water passageways providing maximum freedom of movement in each of the provinces, virtually every farmer learned to fish, sail boats, and trade. People were not bound to their isolated villages and towns, as in much of the rest of Europe. Instead they crossed boundaries to learn the manners and customs of neighboring towns and villages and—later—other countries. Exposed to the world around them, the Dutch kept an open attitude about new ideas.

Water boards, of which hundreds existed as early as 1400, were another way for farmers and citizens to manage their own environment without waiting for approval from higher authorities.

In the cities, people were able to acquire personal freedom in other ways. Booming industry and trade created a class of free traders and artisans. The more powerful these citizens grew, the less they were willing to tolerate the restrictions other countries or cities tried to impose on them. As people gained economic independence, they acquired a taste for personal liberty as well.

Erasmus   Many of the ideas that inspired the Dutch resistance against Spain were articulated much earlier by the philosopher Erasmus. Desiderius Erasmus was born in Rotterdam in 1469. His father was a Roman Catholic priest. Letters Erasmus wrote later in life reveal that he suffered from his illegitimate birth. Neighbors and parishioners must have been scandalized that their priest lived with a woman, and they must have shunned the young Erasmus. His family moved from one town to another and Erasmus grew up in isolation.

Statue of Erasmus in Rotterdam.   Photo from Cas Oorthuys archive

At the age of sixteen Erasmus became a monk. In the monastery he began studying religious literature. The more knowledge he gained, the less satisfied he became with official Roman Catholic doctrine. He came to reject the idea that religion is something to be imposed on an individual and strongly believed that, instead, religious feelings arose from within the person.

After giving up monastic life, Erasmus traveled through Europe. His travels took him to England, France, Italy, Germany, Switzerland, Belgium, and Holland. Although he loved his home country, Erasmus considered himself a citizen of the world. Throughout his life, Erasmus remained a follower of the Catholic faith, although meetings with foreign scientists like Thomas More and John Colet exposed him to the new philosophy of humanism. The humanist philosophers believed that by studying classical Greek and Latin literature and art, people could improve themselves. While they took their inspiration from the ancients, the humanists' belief in self-improvement was a step away from traditional church doctrine.

Erasmus was above all a literary genius, fascinated by the power of the written and spoken word. Seven hundred fifty thousand copies of his books were sold within his own lifetime. In his books Erasmus expressed his contempt for ideological quarrels, believing that people should be guided by reason. His best-known work is *In Praise of Folly* (1509), which exposed the various stupidities of the times: the quackery of physicians, the pettifoggery of the lawyers, the reveling of kings and merchants. Erasmus targeted the abuses committed by the Church and its clergy as well, although he was not a Protestant and also clashed with Luther.

The era in which Erasmus lived was plagued by wars, floods, and human cruelty. Many people felt frightened about what the future might hold. Erasmus shared these fears, but he refused to let them rule him.

Instead, he looked for a balance between fear and a sense of human dignity. Erasmus also criticized war in his writing; this was quite novel in his day.

Erasmus was surprisingly sympathetic toward women, supporting them when men tried to justify their own privileged position by citing the Bible. Erasmus had many logical arguments to use against these men. Picturing difficult situations in his books, he let women play heroic roles negotiating between groggy, panic-stricken men. He calls such women "viragos," which literally means "mannish women." It was his belief that women could very well remain women and show male traits at the same time.

Erasmus was and still is a controversial figure. Some censure him for lacking the courage to take sides; others praise his aloofness and conciliatory spirit.

Protest and Dissension

The most prominent Dutch leader in the Eighty Years War, William of Orange, put Erasmus's words to use in an open letter in which he explained why he would refuse to obey the Spanish King. Every people, he maintained, has the right to rebel against tyranny. Nobody should be persecuted because of his or her religious convictions. This "apologia" (1581) was quickly translated into five languages, and was read with great interest throughout Europe. William's stand inspired others to refuse the King's orders. The Dutch national anthem, which dates from this period, expresses the country's resolve to fight against oppression. The final line of the first stanza calls on the Dutch to "dispel the tyranny that pierces my heart."

The lengthy and bloody conflict with the Spaniards planted deep roots in the Dutch mind. The Dutch nation was born out of protest, and even three centuries later, the Dutch act within that tradition. Protest and demonstrations are still common features of political life in Holland. Modern Dutch law lays down rules for the protection of people who, for instance, have conscientious objections to paying certain taxes or fulfilling military service requirements.

The same spirit of dissension that prevailed in Dutch politics also divided the Dutch in religious matters. In the seventeenth century a slight majority of Netherlanders were Calvinists. One third were Roman Catholics, the remainder being Jews, Lutherans, Mennonites, and atheists. Among the various religious faiths existing in the Netherlands at that time, the Calvinists showed the strongest will to become the official state church. Whether or not this was a good idea, however, kept them so internally divided that their hopes were never realized. Despite this failure, Calvinism and Holland, so it seemed, were made for each other. The Calvinist emphasis on independent thought fit perfectly with the idea of democracy in the Netherlands. The modern German sociologist Max Weber argued in 1905 that the rise of capitalism and the rise of Calvinism were related to each other. The capitalist mind had a relentless drive for accumulating wealth and at the same time was restrained about consuming the fruits of its own labor. Calvinists, Weber said, sought disciplined accumulation as well. Hard work and success provided them with the feeling that they were chosen by God. At the same time they had to remain pure. Earning money and making a profit were not in themselves evil, but woe betide the individual for whom they became the only goal in life.

Fear and Piety

During the Eighty Years War, the Dutch were often torn between two emotions. On the one hand, they were courageous enough to control the sea, to resist the powerful Spaniards, and to build an economic empire.

On the other hand, they were afraid. The sea, the Spanish, as well as disease and crime, were all formidable enemies. Tossed between courage and fear, Dutch citizens gradually looked to religion as a source of strength. God had helped the Dutch, as many people believed, to master the sea and to accumulate their massive wealth and power. Now they hoped God would help them in defeating the Spaniards. Church ministers preached from their pulpits the comforting news that God had chosen the Dutch people as he had once chosen the people of Israel. Like Israel, the Dutch would be forced to endure great hardship. But in the end, so the ministers prophesied, they would be liberated. The Dutch, in turn, were expected to live by God's commandments. Only then would God protect them.

A clear illustration of the fear and piety prevalent in those days is revealed in the diary of Johan Bontekoe. Published for the first time in 1646, the book quickly became a best-seller, eventually reprinted seventy times. One adventure depicted in Captain Bontekoe's diary is a devastating fire at sea, on board his ship *De Nieuw Hoorn* (*The New Horn*, named after the Dutch town of Hoorn). The enormous ship, comparable in size with today's ocean liners, exploded. Bontekoe was wounded, pulled himself onto a piece of floating wreckage, and together with surviving crew members, was lost at sea for weeks. Rescue seemed unlikely, and the survivors' hunger grew worse each day. The men decided that they would start eating the cabin boys if land was not reached within three days. Bontekoe's entry for that day reads:

The urgency was so great that we were not able to endure it much longer. We were constantly thinking: If we could just get to land, then we could at least eat grass, there wouldn't be any problem. I comforted the men, as much as lay in my power. I told them they would have to maintain strong courage, that the Lord would ensure that everything would take a turn for the better; but I myself was lacking in courage, perhaps able to comfort another, but had the need to be comforted myself!

Two days later, land was finally sighted. A jubilant Bontekoe wrote:

We immediately set sail again and sailed toward the land, touching the ground on that very same day. We believed in and praised the almighty Lord who had heard our prayers and pleading; because we prayed mornings as well as nights with a fiery devotion to God, and sang as well a psalm before and after the prayer.

Stories like Bontekoe's—filled with good and evil, heroes and villains—were popular not only because they evoked a sense of adventure and excitement, but also because they provided a reassuring resolution of life's problems.

The Thinkers

Religion in the Netherlands was increasingly influenced by humanism. Following in the footsteps of Erasmus, the writer Dirck Volckertsz Coornhert (1522–1590) raised fundamental questions about religion and morality. He was a religious man, but not a churchgoing man. He found he was able to read the Bible without a minister's advice. Coornhert's greatest contribution to Dutch culture was his appeal for tolerance and freedom of conscience. Believing that religious disputes could be fought only with words and not with weapons, Coornhert went a step further than Erasmus and disassociated himself entirely from the quarreling Protestants and Roman Catholics.

In his own time, Erasmus had called for international collaboration. Appalled by the cruelties of his epoch, he rejected the idea that war was an inevitable evil. People, he had said, could be improved by education. International conferences could keep humanity from destroying itself. People would benefit "from the advice of learned men." Some fifty years later another Dutch genius, Huig de Groot (1583–1645), elaborated on Erasmus's ideas. De Groot, also called Hugo Grotius, was a man with a brilliant and versatile mind. He began his university studies at the age of eleven and, five years later, earned his first doctorate. De Groot would later become an attorney, a playwright, theologian, translator, and diplomat. In his *Mare Liberum* (*Freedom of the Seas*), he held that no single country should be permitted full control of the seas. He pleaded in favor of free trade between all countries. In his best-known work, *De Jure Belli et Pacis* (*On the Law of War and Peace*, 1625) de Groot maintained that war should be fought only on fair terms. Violence was to be used only in a limited number of cases: in self-defense, to regain stolen assets, and to punish injustice "within the limits of law and good faith." When sovereigns or nations clashed, a supreme, international legal system should be in place in order to judge disputes. De Groot's book was to lay the foundation for modern international law, which in turn paved the way for the United Nations.

The Masters

In the Golden Age, the Dutch enjoyed a relatively high degree of freedom of speech. Officially authorities possessed the power of censorship, but in practice plenty of room remained to evade the rules. Many books banned in other countries were freely published in the Netherlands. The philosopher Baruch—or Benedict—Spinoza (1632–1677), a Portuguese Jew whose parents had fled from Portugal to Amsterdam, felt free to publish his radical ideas in the Netherlands. Spinoza's work on ethics was inspired by Dutch teachers and fit with the liberal atmosphere of his surroundings. He praised those who were guided by reason rather than being slaves to their emotions.

As influential and popular as these books from the Golden Age of Holland might be among scholars, they have not gained half as much fame and recognition as the Dutch painting of the period. Dutch masters such as Rembrandt van Rijn, Frans Hals, Johannes Vermeer, Jan Steen, Jacob and Salomon van Ruisdael, Meindert Hobbema, and Paulus Potter have received worldwide recognition, sometimes more today than in their own time.

For years art historians claimed that painters in Holland and Italy, where some of the best European artists lived in this period, used very different means to render physical reality. In Italy, most painters worked for the Roman Catholic Church and for various local rulers. The decoration of churches and palaces was their main occupation. Often a realistic representation of landscapes, buildings, and people was not their primary goal. The settings of many Italian paintings, for example, were chosen freely by the artist to suit a particular theme. A biblical story might be depicted in an Italian landscape.

Painters in the Republic of the Seven United Netherlands worked in a very different environment. Assignments were rarely received from the royal court or the churches. A painter in Holland was simply a craftsperson, often forced to take on extra work beyond painting to earn a living.

Johannes Vermeer (1632–1675), whose paintings are worth millions of dollars today, could not make a living from his artwork. A shop inherited from his father provided for his regular income; in his remaining hours he worked, slowly and meticulously, on his paintings. The clients of Jan Steen (1626–1679) were mainly sailors, peasants, and ordinary citizens, who regarded his work as just another piece of furniture.

Rembrandt van Rijn (1606–1669) was one of the few painters who were not satisfied with the modest status of Dutch artists. When his work began to attract attention, he moved from Leiden to Amsterdam, hoping to become part of high society there. At the very height of his glory he married Saskia van Uylenburgh, the daughter of a wealthy

The Love Letter. *A woman, apparently in love, on the verge of opening a letter delivered to her by a maid. Many Dutch seventeenth-century paintings are more than a straightforward portrayal of reality. All kinds of symbols are hidden in the tableaux. Here a woman sits reading a letter near the window. The painting on the wall shows a small boat on a stormy sea. In Vermeer's time, a boat on a rough sea was a well-known symbol: It referred to the uncertainty of human life. It may also mean that her beloved is far away at sea.* Painting by Johannes Vermeer, 1658. Photo by Rijksmuseum, Amsterdam

citizen. Now he could lead an exciting life among "the rich and famous" of Amsterdam. His famous *The Night Watch*—an assignment from the "security police" of Amsterdam—yielded the largest sum of money paid for a painting in those days in Holland.

The painting *Rembrandt and Saskia*, in which he has portrayed himself as a richly clothed, lavish tippler, used to be seen as proof of the exuberant life Rembrandt led during this period. More recently it has been shown that Rembrandt made the painting as a "moral lesson" in which he warned other people and probably also himself against this way of life.

The Company of Captain Frans Banning Cocq, *now known as* The Night Watch. Painting by Rembrandt van Rijn, 1642. Photo by Rijksmuseum, Amsterdam

National Sin

Paintings showing drunken people were not unusual in seventeenth-century Holland, since there were so many drunken people to paint.

Some historians have called excessive drinking the "national sin" of the republic in the seventeenth century. An Italian visitor reported that he was not amazed women played a prominent role in households and business, since "men are drunk most of the time." And an Englishman wrote: "Where ever you look, you meet shippers speaking with a thick tongue, and you see intoxicated people, sitting on the box of a carriage. If something goes wrong in Holland, there's always the excuse of excessive drinking. Judges even take the drinking into account in their judgments."

In 1613, Amsterdam alone had 518 drinking places, one for every two hundred inhabitants. In these drinking places—the predecessors of the modern cafés—customers drank enormous amounts of alcohol, mainly beer and Holland gin. On average each Netherlander drank 264 quarts (250 liters) of beer each year. The upper class preferred wine, something the poor people could not afford. There was a legitimate reason for drinking beer: It was healthier than drinking water, which was often polluted. But drinking alcohol was, of course, also a way to forget about pain and daily trouble.

In the end, Rembrandt returned to the seclusion in which he had started his career. He grew bored with the kinds of pictures people wanted him to paint. Instead, he chose themes and styles that pleased himself. By following this course, his main sources of income dried up, until he was finally declared bankrupt in 1656. Rembrandt's reputation endured, but he died a poor man.

In seventeenth-century Holland, painting was very much part of daily life. Travelers from abroad were amazed. Everywhere they looked—in bakeries, butchers' shops, kitchens—there were paintings. About two hundred years later the same paintings became valuable to wealthy art collectors. American bankers and industrialists—Henry Frick, J. Pier-

The Battle of the Downs against the Spanish Armada, 21 October 1639. *(1659). The Eighty Years War: the Dutch admiral Maarten Harpertszoon Tromp defeats with thirteen ships a mighty Spanish fleet made up of seventy-seven ships and 20,000 men. Van de Velde made his sea paintings using a small boat provided by the Dutch government as a model.* Drawing by Willem van de Velde de Oude. Photo by Rijksmuseum, Amsterdam

pont Morgan, Andrew Mellon—bought many such paintings and took them home. Today more work of Dutch masters is in American than in Dutch possession.

For Americans Dutch paintings also had political value. The Dutch revolt against absolutist forces was similar to their own struggle for freedom and democratic principles. "In love of liberty and in the defense of it, Holland has been our example," Benjamin Franklin said at the height of that struggle.

Dutch paintings in this period seem to be precise pictures of real situations, very different from the fantasies of their Italian counterparts. However, recent research has shown that Dutch paintings are replete with symbols and hidden meanings. While the style in which they are rendered looks more "realistic" than that of the Italians, the Dutch paintings contain religious, poetic, and moral messages. Both Italian and Dutch paintings reflect the beliefs and ideas that shaped people's thinking in the seventeenth century. Neither is perfectly "realistic."

Modern History

With the signing of the Treaty of Munster ending the Eighty Years War in 1648, the Republic of the Seven United Netherlands was officially recognized by other countries as an independent state. Not only was the republic independent, it was strong. And this was a new kind of strength for a country: Instead of basing its power on armies, the strength of this new nation was built on trade.

The Dutch rise to power paralleled the emergence, for the first time in European history, of a real global market. Previous European centers of commerce—Venice, Genoa, Lisbon, Bruges, Antwerp—traded only in limited regions of the world. With the rise of Holland and, in particular, of Amsterdam, trade became a global affair and would remain so from that day forward.

The Dutch reached the height of their power by about 1660. From that time on, their empire began to wane. The country remained as wealthy as it was before, but in relative terms it lost ground to other states. On the one hand, England was eager to take over Holland's leading commercial position; on the other hand, the French King Louis XIV repeatedly tried to annex the southern provinces. The republic was involved in an exhausting series of conflicts. Motivated by rivalry over trade, England undertook four maritime wars against the Netherlands. Although the first war was indecisive and the second one was gloriously won by the Dutch, the third and fourth wars caused Holland to give up considerable parts of its colonial and naval power.

The republic and England really had a love-hate relationship during these centuries. In the years between the wars both countries repeatedly collaborated as allies. The chief common interest of both countries was to check the ambitions of France. In the 1680's British Protestants feared that their own Roman Catholic King, James II, might destroy their church with the help of the French King Louis XIV, a confirmed believer in the supremacy of the Roman Catholic faith. The Protestants called for the help of the Dutch Prince William III of Orange. William was the husband of James II's daughter Mary and *stadtholder*, as the highest official was called, of the republic. William accepted the invitation. In November 1688, masses of spectators along the channel coast saw a mighty fleet pass: five hundred carrier ships, surrounded by sixty warships, ten fireboats, and many small vessels. In the vanguard sailed the flagship, carrying the coats of arms of William and Mary and the motto "For Liberty and Protestant Religion, Je Maintiendrai" (French for: I will maintain). That same year the bloodless "Glorious Revolution" took place: The Protestant William and Mary were crowned King and Queen of England and James II fled to France. But their power was limited. Along with the new royal family came a Bill of Rights and a larger role for parliament. Now the time was ripe for an attack on the French King. From 1688 until 1697 the War of the Grand Alliance took place, in which the English and Dutch, joined by other European nations, fought against France. Since William and Mary had no children, England and the Netherlands remained distinct nations with their own rulers.

The last war the Anglo-Dutch forces fought against France ended in the treaties of Utrecht (1713) and Rastadt (1714), in which the republic did not make out well. Dutch independence was preserved and France was kept out of Flanders, but England had gradually surpassed its ally in trade and naval power. London, not Amsterdam, was the focal point of world trade now. Furthermore, the provinces were compelled to devote the greater part of their energies to guarding their southern borders to prevent new French intrusions.

The Dutch *regenten* (the wealthy upper class) eventually became less willing to make new sacrifices. They were settled now and opted for safe investment in land or state securities. They had little taste for hazardous commercial or military ventures. When new conflicts between England and France arose later in the eighteenth century, the republic remained neutral.

Political Crisis

Toward the end of the eighteenth century, the Netherlands entered a new period, marked by a long political crisis (1780–1848). Many people began to feel that affluent families and descendants of the Orange dynasty were doing a bad job of governing the republic. Much to their distress, there seemed to be no alternative. The question of who should govern the country remained unanswered. As the Dutch faced this internal conflict, international conditions were changing. The Seven

United Netherlands' southern neighbor, France, had long been a formidable nation headed by an absolute monarch. But in the late eighteenth century it entered a period of crisis. New ideals of liberty, equality, and fraternity, as well as declining economic conditions, inspired French revolutionaries to attempt to create a new state in which rational government would replace inherited authority. Comparable revolutions were taking place in other regions of the world, including North America. Historians see these changes as part of an "Atlantic Revolution": Revolutionaries in France and the United States were fighting for the same ideals at the same time. In the Republic of the Seven United Netherlands this revolution was embraced by the *Patriotten* (Patriots). The Patriots were troubled by the country's apparent lack of political advancement. Political authority was still apportioned to individual provinces and towns, with no strong central government. The Patriots hoped the French Revolution would set a new example for their own society.

By the time the French reached the republic, however, the revolutionary movement had been overtaken by conservative forces. A new military leader, named Napoleon Bonaparte, was on the rise. In 1795 a French army crossed the frozen rivers of the United Netherlands and encountered little resistance. A new French-style "Batavian Republic" was established by the Napoleonic government. Vital innovations such as the postal system and a standard monetary unit were introduced. Streets were provided with names, houses with numbers. All citizens, who were formerly called son or daughter of so-and-so, received official family names, which were to be entered in a national registry. Weights and measures were systematized, as were civil and criminal legal codes. The French domination seemed to provide the country with the structure it needed so badly. But the independent-minded Dutch soon became impatient with the authoritarianism of the Napoleonic regime. In 1810 the French decided that the United Netherlands could be run more efficiently as a French province. Harsh oppression was used to stem political protests against this move. Moreover, a new French tax system was introduced, clearly intended to transfer as much Dutch money as possible to France. Dutch commerce had also been severely hurt by a French embargo against trade with England. By the time the Napoleonic empire collapsed in 1815 and the French withdrew from the Netherlands, Dutch citizens were happy to see them go.

King of the Netherlands

The Patriots' hopes had not been realized: The French had not provided the country with a solution to its political crisis. In an attempt to bring order to the country, a constitution was introduced and accepted in 1815. This constitution permanently abolished the former powers of the provinces and established a new central monarchy, which included both the northern and the southern provinces. William I, a descendant of William of Orange's brother, assumed the title "King of the Netherlands." William, also called the "merchant King," governed the country energetically. His assertive campaign to reinforce Dutch industry and transportation created networks of canals that soon became vital passages linking cities like Amsterdam and Rotterdam with the sea.

During the first ten years the joining of northern and southern provinces seemed to work. But King William's style of governing did not please everyone. William was a curt and stubborn man. Moreover, he liked to stress the supremacy of the Holland region and of Calvinism. Differences in religious belief and language between north and south reemerged. Episcopal schools in the south refused to teach their pupils the Dutch language, a decision that greatly angered Dutch Calvinists. People in the south started to call themselves Belgians, the French word for Netherlanders. When, in 1830, riots broke out in several southern cities, the pressure on the Dutch King mounted.

At last he conceded the inevitability of secession. In 1839 a declaration was signed confirming the creation of two independent countries: Belgium and the Netherlands. Flanders and the southern half of the Brabant province became parts of Belgium. The Luxemburg province, a grand duchy, remained linked with the Netherlands since the grand ducal title belonged to the House of Orange. During the following decades, however, Luxemburg signed treaties with Belgium and Germany, loosening its historical ties with the Netherlands. The northern provinces expanded their territory. Large parts of Brabant and Limburg were added to the original seven provinces. The name "the Netherlands" was now reserved for this new territory.

To provide the people a sense of unity, the government of the Netherlands started a propaganda campaign in which it insistently put forth the argument that the new Netherlands was a direct continuation of the Netherlands as it had been during the Burgundian period. The campaign was quite effective. A growing number of people came to accept the idea that their country had simply reformed its original borders and that there was no more important value than fidelity to God and justice. The old feeling of being a chosen people returned. The image of a small and defenseless, but morally impeccable, people was restored once again.

A New Constitution

In the independent Netherlands, a new constitution was introduced in 1848 to counterbalance the king's authority. The originator of the constitution, the liberal scientist and politician Johan Rudolf Thorbecke, compared society to the human body: Every organ has its own character and function, yet they are all related to each other. Inspired by this model, he divided central power among the king, a cabinet of ministers, and a parliament. Acts would still have to be signed by the king, but would require the signature of the appropriate minister as well. Ministers would bear the responsibility for any bill made into law. In turn, all decisions and actions of the minister would be checked by parliament. The lower house was granted important democratic rights. All meetings of parliament were opened to the public.

The new constitution left many citizens politically disadvantaged. The right to vote had been granted only to citizens who paid at least a specified amount in taxes. Newly created political parties called for an electoral system that would make all men and women eligible for the vote and eligible as candidates. Catholics and orthodox Protestants were no longer satisfied with their limited role in society. They demanded that their schools receive state subsidies.

Abraham Kuyper and His Ordinary People

The shape of Dutch society has been strongly influenced by the ideas of Abraham Kuyper, nicknamed "The Terrific" (1837–1920). This son of a preacher was obsessed by the idea of creating a network of Protestant strongholds within Dutch society. He rejected the liberal society that had arisen after the introduction of Thorbecke's constitution. The freethinking atmosphere curtailed, in his opinion, the rights of religious people.

Kuyper started his career as a village preacher but soon extended his influence well beyond the village borders by publishing attention-getting articles in a national church magazine. His fame spread quickly and soon he became the leader of the small Anti-Revolutionaire Partij (Anti-Revolutionary Party), in which the orthodox members of the Calvinist churches had united. As a political leader and a member of parliament, he transformed the party into a powerful, nationwide organization.

Abraham Kuyper, nicknamed "The Terrific" (1837–1920). Illustration by Albert Hahn

In every corner of the country, Kuyper attracted crowds, sharing his ideas with a breathless public of ordinary people—mainly workers, clerks, shop owners, and farmers. It was not his intention to overturn the social order, he said. He did not want to replace liberalism but just demanded room for other, competing groups. Christians should have the opportunity to lead their lives according to the Bible and to the rules of their own church.

On Kuyper's initiative Protestants insisted on their right to governmental funding for their own schools. By concentrating on this sensitive topic, he was able to forge alliances with other religious groups. The Roman Catholics, for instance, saw good reasons now to found their own political party, the Katholieke Volkspartij (Catholic People's Party). In the end, the founding of schools and universities based on religion or philosophy of life was recognized as a social right. In every town and district, Roman Catholic, Protestant, and nonsectarian schools were built beside each other, all fully supported by government funding. Every school worked hard to teach its pupils its own particular view of the world. For Kuyper this was not enough. First he helped create the influential daily newspaper *De Standaard* (*The Standard*), then he organized a scientific institute and several social associations. Finally, in 1888, he established in Amsterdam a Protestant university called the Vrije Universiteit (Free University).

In the same year, the Anti-Revolutionary Party and the Catholic People's Party together won a majority in parliament for the first time. Now poor people, farmers, and small businesspeople had their share of power. Although Kuyper's sturdy combative style did not please everyone, he became Prime Minister in 1901. Now Kuyper showed the limits of his tolerance. He ordered, for instance, a ban on homosexuality and introduced a law that declared all strikes of civil servants illegal. After four years his prime ministery was over. But Kuyper remained active, and when he died in 1920 his ideal, the pillarization of society along religious lines (see Chapter 8), had found a permanent base.

Parliament was simultaneously faced with other urgent issues. Factories prospered thanks to laborers' efforts, but should twelve- or four-teen-hour work days be tolerated? Was child labor an inhumane practice? Should compulsory education be introduced? Ethical discussions regarding the Dutch colonies also arose: Were the East Indies and the Antilles solely there for the benefit of the mother country or should these territories be granted aid for their own development?

Under the initiative of a progressive member of parliament, legislation was passed in 1874 that prohibited the employment of children

Max Havelaar

The East Indies, the vast archipelago in Southeast Asia, were as much a part of a proud Dutch self-image as they were a part of the Dutch empire. The Indies were ruled by governors and civil servants from Holland. Local economic resources—rubber, tobacco, coffee, oil, and spices—had been exploited by Dutch companies for many years. The East Indies were also very much a part of Dutch literature. The twelve-volume *Library of the Indies* presents in English translation books that reflect Dutch people's experiences in the tropical islands. The most celebrated volume in the series is the novel *Max Havelaar.*

The story is based on the life of Multatuli (the pen name of Eduard Douwes Dekker). Douwes Dekker (1820–1887) migrated from Holland to the Indies in 1838. Officially appointed as Resident Assistant, he experienced directly the exploitation of the Asian population. He found that workers were not paid for their labor and were victimized by blackmail and other abuses of power. A rebellious idealist, Douwes Dekker challenged the local authorities. But all his efforts were suppressed. Isolated and disillusioned, he returned to Europe. In 1859, while staying at a poor boarding house in Brussels, he wrote his novel *Max Havelaar* in only one month. In it he not only described the injustices of the Dutch colonial administration, but also held a mirror up to the self-satisfied people at home who had closed their eyes to this exploitation.

Max Havelaar has been translated into twenty-four languages including English and has exerted a considerable influence on Dutch politics and morality.

under twelve years of age. Other bills followed, some of them stirring considerable controversy. The Franchise Act (1894) allowed all male citizens capable of supporting their families to vote. The Act provoked opposition among a small group of women. The driving force behind them was Aletta Jacobs. As a doctor she had reproached her male colleagues for the neglectful way they treated prostitutes, even when these women were dangerously ill. She had criticized her colleagues' theory that men could be healthy only if they satisfied their sexual desires with as many healthy women as possible. And, what was even more daring, she brought up the subject of birth control, pleading for the right of women to choose for themselves whether to be mothers. In 1903, she became the leader of the Association for Female Suffrage. Envisioning the day on which women could vote, she wrote:

Then it will become clear which power is carried by a simple ballot, how all our social action will progress ten times quicker, how social evils will disappear under our influence—evils that could spread for centuries because everywhere and in all matters the female hand, and above all, the female heart, was lacking.

Jacobs became the champion of female suffrage and gathered a movement around her that formed the "first feminist wave," as it is called today. In 1919 parliament passed the Jacobs Act, introducing female suffrage to the Netherlands.

Around the turn of the century, when the socialist movement and trade unions gained a foothold in the Netherlands—much later than in other European countries—other social questions were resolved in rapid succession. The Compulsory Education Act was passed in 1900, the Industrial Injuries Insurance Act, Health Act, and Housing Act in 1901. The relative ease with which Holland managed to find answers for its internal debates was remarkable. Tolerance and a sense of pluralism now helped solve the problems faced by many industrial nations.

As the center of world influence shifted away from the Netherlands, Dutch foreign policy became more modest than it had ever been. Holland had seldom—the East Indies being a notable exception—been interested in military conquest and territorial expansion; it had primarily sought commercial expansion. Holland now pleaded more actively for compromise as a way to preserve a stable and peaceful international order. This attitude was based less on high-minded principles than on enlightened self-interest: The Netherlands' survival had grown to depend almost entirely on solid working relationships with its neighbors.

Holland upheld its policy of neutrality well into the twentieth century. When World War I broke out in 1914, the Netherlands did not take sides. Neighboring countries, including Belgium, suffered heavily, but life in Holland went on as usual, and its economy even prospered. Holland's hopes for a safe niche in world politics were brutally crushed, however, when, in 1940, World War II crossed Dutch borders.

World War II

Adolf Hitler's invasion of Holland in 1940 caught the Dutch people unaware. Or perhaps they wanted to be unaware. Accustomed to their neutrality, they had given little attention to the maintenance of an efficient army. Soldiers were poorly trained. Artillery dated back to the period of World War I: The country possessed no modern tanks, and several cannons had to be taken from the army museum. The bicycle was still a common army vehicle.

The German army attacked with full force on May 10, 1940. In the early morning, paratroopers landed near military airports in the coastal provinces and put the Dutch air force almost completely out of action. Although in some strategic locations the Dutch were able to hold back the German forces, the advance soon proved to be unstoppable. The Hague, where the seat of government and the royal residence were located, came under attack.

But the Germans dealt their most decisive blow with the bombing of the city of Rotterdam. The city's center was completely destroyed. Nine hundred people were killed and the homes of an additional 78,500 were destroyed. The Dutch signed a statement of capitulation on May 15. In the meantime Queen Wilhelmina and many governmental officials fled to England.

Initially, the Germans handled the Dutch with kid gloves. Winning the cooperation of the Dutch people, they hoped, would make it easier to integrate Holland into the German empire. The reality, however, was that there were few admirers of Germany in Holland.

One movement that was particularly outspoken in its sympathy for the Germans was the Nationaal Socialistische Beweging (National Socialist Movement). Its Fascist leader, Anton Mussert, had visions of participating in a German empire well before the Germans invaded the Netherlands. He himself would rule over the "Greater Netherlands," comprising Holland, the Flemish part of Belgium, and the Dutch East India colonies. The Germans granted Mussert's National Socialist Movement permission to be active as a political party, but did not give him the role he envisioned. The party remained isolated and was disdained by many Dutch people. When the war broke out, the party listed 33,000 members. By 1941 this number had grown to 87,000, but total membership never exceeded 1 percent of the population.

In the first year of the war, most Dutch people preferred to avoid actively supporting or clearly opposing the Nazis. Some made an attempt to reconcile themselves to the German presence, wanting to believe that nothing had really changed in the aftermath of the attack. Yet a flood of new members to a newly formed political movement suggested the public's feeling, however vague, that "something had to happen." The Dutch Union, formed in May 1940, did not share the ideas of the Nazis but did recommend cooperation with them. Union leaders believed that a constructive relationship with the Germans could be worked out. When the first signs of resistance appeared—a shooting or an illegal leaflet—the Union's leadership was quick to disassociate itself from these illegal activities.

The Jewish Tragedy

By 1941 the Nazis' step-by-step campaign against the Jewish population began. Initially, Jews were restricted to areas designated as non-Aryan. Jewish people were denied access to certain streets and were forbidden to enter movie houses, ride bicycles, or use public transportation. For identification, all Jews were forced to wear large yellow stars on their clothing.

In the second phase of the campaign Jews were systematically deported, first to transitory camps elsewhere in Holland. From there trains loaded with Jews left every week for extermination camps in Germany, Austria, and Poland. Most of the deported people died in the gas chambers. Others were beaten to death or died from hunger and fatigue. By the end of the war, 107,000 Dutch Jews—of a prewar population of 140,000—had been annihilated. Only 5,200 Dutch Jews survived the extermination camps. Non-Jewish Dutch families, willing to put their own lives at risk, managed to hide an estimated 25,000 Jews from the Germans. Several thousand Jews managed to escape to other countries.

The diaries of Anne Frank and Etty Hillesum reflect those difficult times and show how some Jewish people lived and struggled during the war.

Jewish people hiding from the Germans.   Photo from Cas Oorthuys archive

Anne Frank was four years old when she and her parents left Nazi Germany. In Amsterdam, their new home, the Frank family tried to build a new life. In July 1942, however, German anti-Semitic activities intensified. The family had no other option but to go into hiding. For more than two years, Anne, her family, and some friends took secret refuge in a house in Amsterdam, living under the same difficult conditions as the 25,000 other Jews hiding in Holland.

Anne kept a diary of this time. Entries were addressed to a fictitious friend named Kitty. "With writing I can let everything out," she said. The diary shows that Anne was aware of what was happening to other Jews: "We assume that most of them are killed. The English radio talks about gas chambers. Maybe that's the quickest way of dying. I'm completely upset." The diary ends just before the family's deportation to a concentration camp in Germany. Someone had betrayed their hiding place.

Anne wrote several short stories during those two years. In one story, "Fear" (written March 25, 1944), she recounts a dream. Her house has been bombed. She dreams that she runs away until finally she reaches a meadow:

I looked up into the sky and realized that I was no longer afraid; on the contrary, I felt very peaceful inside. The funny thing was that I didn't think of my family, nor yearn for them; I yearned only for rest, and it wasn't long before I fell asleep there in the grass, under the sky.

Movie-star stills on the wall of the room in which Anne Frank hid before she was discovered by the Nazis.   Particam Pictures

Anne died at the age of fifteen at the concentration camp Bergen-Belsen. After the war her diary was translated into more than thirty languages. The house in Amsterdam where she and her family hid is now the Anne Frank Museum.

The diary of Etty Hillesum, published in English in 1981 as *An Interrupted Life*, presents a more philosophical view of this period. Hillesum was less concerned with the daily events of her life. She wrote primarily about her own reactions to the hatred and aggression she encountered. Should she resist? Should she try to escape? Hillesum's conclusion was that the noblest solution was to learn to accept her suffering. For her, the person who refuses to play the part of the victim is the real victor.

The Resistance

By 1941, a growing number of Dutch people began to feel that cooperating with the Germans was neither right nor practical. The United States' entry into the war also sparked hopes that the Germans could be defeated. In February of that year, the first deportations of Jews prompted a spontaneous general strike by workers in Amsterdam. An underground resistance movement, composed of small, independent units, became active. The groups attacked and destroyed population registers, where the names of all citizens were listed. With these lists in hand the Nazis could determine which people might be in hiding. Resisters liberated colleagues from prison and assassinated collaborators. The groups' potential, however, was limited. Holland, with so many people on so little, and such flat, land, was not the ideal place for a full-scale partisan war. The Germans were firmly retaliating against every act of resistance. Dutch people were arbitrarily being taken hostage and executed in reaction to any kind of anti-German activity.

Resistance workers duplicating an illegal newspaper (1944).   Photo from Cas Oorthuys
archive

On a broader scale, people were involved in peaceful resistance. The
production and distribution of underground papers, for example, flourished. By the end of the war, more than a thousand journals were being
printed. Copies were distributed by thousands of people who, despite
hardly knowing each other, formed secret networks. One copy of a piece
of underground writing might be circulated to a hundred people or

more, each of whom knew only the person he or she got it from and the person who was next on the list. Some papers were published occasionally, others on a more regular basis. The newspaper *Het Parool* (*The Watchword*), founded in 1940, circulated more than 100,000 copies during the last year of the war. Today it is still one of the leading Dutch newspapers. Other current dailies and weeklies, like *Trouw* (*Fidelity*) and *Vrij Nederland* (*Free Netherlands*), were originally illegal newspapers.

The Last Winter

The end of the war was a long and dark period in Dutch history. Many precious days passed before the Allied troops reached Holland after the invasion of Normandy on June 6, 1944. On September 17 of that year, the great day appeared to have arrived. In one massive attack called "Operation Market Garden," British, American, and Polish troops set out to capture a chain of strategic points and bridges in the south of Holland. Probably due to Allied miscalculations, however, an attack at the Rhine crossing near Arnhem failed utterly. *A Bridge Too Far*, as the bridge is called in the film of the same name, was unexpectedly defended by a heavily armored German *panzer* (tank) corps. Seventy-six hundred of the ten thousand Allied paratroopers were killed. Only six hundred soldiers reached the bridge. The bridge was not taken.

By the winter of that same year, northern Holland was still under occupation. To tighten its control, German forces cut off the Randstad's food supply. In a winter that will never be forgotten by the Dutch, a terrible famine hit the cities in the west. Many died of starvation and exhaustion. Holland was not freed until the following spring, on May 5, 1945. By that time, the war had taken the lives of 280,000 Dutch people, including Jews, and left behind millions of painful memories.

The famine in the winter of 1944–1945 drove thousands of people from the Randstad into the countryside in search for food.   Photo from Cas Oorthuys archive

Since the war fear of new conflicts and support for pacifism have grown in Holland. On the other hand, many feel that Holland needs a strong army to keep new enemies from attacking again.

The Dutch are still not sure whether to feel proud or ashamed of their actions during the war. Each year around May 4—the national day of commemoration—and May 5—Liberation Day—new debates are set off that invariably end in controversy or uncertainty. Some press stories and TV documentaries stress the heroic nature of the resistance and strikes against the Germans or highlight the help that was given to the Jews. More skeptical people, however, argue that an overwhelming

1990. Near the porch of the Prime Minister's house, a woman weeps upon hearing the news that two German prisoners of war will be released.   Photo by Werry Crone/Trouw

majority of the Dutch, when they had gotten over their initial fears, behaved as if nothing serious was going on. They also point to the fact that only a fraction of the population was actively involved in the resistance and that for four years trains taking Jews to their death left the country on schedule and unimpeded. The question of who was "good" or "bad" during the war has been an ongoing concern for the Dutch, one still reflected in new novels and feature films. Even in recent years the revelation of new facts about people's behavior during the war years has led to ruined careers and public disgrace.

Loss of Colonies

Holland had no rest after the war. Action was required on two fronts. At home, the restoration of the ravaged country and its economy was carried out rapidly and successfully. A second task, in the Orient, was handled with less skill. During the war a strong nationalistic movement had arisen in the Indonesian colonies. With the war over, this movement demanded that the Dutch withdraw and recognize an independent Indonesian Republic. The Netherlands initially refused. Few could imagine a Holland without the rich and beautiful archipelago that had become a part of people's collective memories and the Dutch identity. There was also an underlying fear that losing the Indies would signal the former superpower's final decline to the level of a third-rate state. Powerful Dutch economic interests were also at stake. More than five hundred Dutch companies, among them giants like Unilever and Shell, were located in the Indies.

Holland undertook peaceful, diplomatic maneuvers to "protect" the islands against "the nationalist threat," but simultaneously sent more than a hundred thousand Dutch soldiers to the other end of the globe to, if necessary, defend the colonies with military force. As a final decision seemed inevitable, public emotions grew heated. The Indonesia question split Holland into opposing camps. Indonesia's struggle for independence resulted in two military confrontations (in 1947 and 1948), the loss of many lives, and considerable pressure from other Western countries. Finally, in 1949 the Republic of Indonesia was granted independence by the Dutch government. Holland was initially permitted to keep one foothold on Indonesian territory, on West Irian, but was later forced to give up that base as well in 1963.

Since Indonesian independence, the Netherlands has modified its colonial ties with less controversy. The Latin American colony of Suri-

Armed Dutch planter at his East Indies estate (1947).   Photo from Cas Oorthuys archive

nam became an independent republic in 1975. At present six Antillean islands off the Venezuelan coast remain overseas possessions of the Kingdom of the Netherlands.

After World War II the position of the Netherlands changed profoundly. The policy of neutrality had to be abandoned. The country was forced to take sides. First it became a member of the North Atlantic Treaty Organization (NATO) in 1949. Later, in 1957, it was one of the cofounders of the European Economic Community (EEC). In 1990 Holland actively participated in the military coalition against Iraq, although its contribution was relatively small. The once-mighty colonial power has become a minor participant in world politics, a member of larger organizations that must fight to preserve its position and identity.

An Amazing Economy

Holland is no longer a worldwide empire. The country's old economic mainstay, the shipping trade, has almost completely disappeared. Yet Holland appears to have entered a new Golden Age in the late twentieth century. With only 14,000 square miles (36,200 square kilometers) of Dutch territory, the country can boast the world's busiest port, Europe's leading transportation companies, record-breaking crops, and the headquarters of some of the world's most prominent multinational corporations. Today more than three quarters of what the Dutch produce is exported. Holland is the world's biggest exporter of refined oil products, vegetables, dairy products, meat and poultry, flowers, and cacao products. The country has a highly developed economy, built around strong industry. The working population possesses a sound work ethic, its management a good sense for organization.

The Dutch: Where Do and Did They Work?

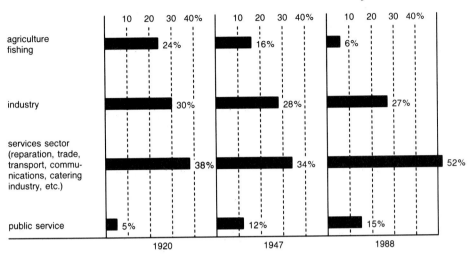

In the shadow of this success, however, 800,000 Dutch households earn a minimal income and enjoy little of the country's prosperity. These people usually live in small rental homes with barely enough money for food and clothing. The percentage of absent and disabled workers is much higher in the Netherlands than in surrounding countries. Living up to the country's high standards takes its toll.

Some regions share in the general prosperity less than others. The west, including the cities of Rotterdam, Amsterdam, and The Hague, is the country's economic stronghold. But unemployment in the northern province of Groningen, a region severely behind in economic development, ranks very high. One out of every five of its citizens is unable to find work. Many young people leave Groningen in search of better educational or employment opportunities in the central or western provinces. Economic growth in the southern province of North Brabant, however, has been spectacular. Expanding industry in these cities provides new jobs for people willing to move. Eindhoven, where the headquarters of Philips are located, is a major industrial and research center.

Church and Commerce

Rijnsburg is a middle-sized town near the coast of Holland. After Aalsmeer and Westland, the two competing Dutch flower regions, Rijnsburg holds the largest cut-flower auction in the world. Its citizens, for the most part members of reformed Protestant churches, reserve Sundays for church and rest. On Monday morning, however, economic life resumes its dynamic pace. At half past six in the morning, the town's auction hall is packed with buyers and a rich variety of flowers, which have been carefully cultivated in local greenhouses (a Dutch invention). There is an endless array of flowers of every size, color, and smell, with 4.8 million flowers changing hands every working day. Within hours of a sale, airplanes and trucks deliver the flowers to destinations around the world.

Approximately 85 percent of Rijnsburg's working population is involved with the cultivation and trading of cut flowers. Plenty of jobs are available, and enthusiasm for the work is high. Few receive unemployment compensation in Rijnsburg.

On a small scale, Rijnsburg reflects important traditional values in the Dutch economy. As mentioned earlier, the preacher and the merchant were role models for Dutch society. Rijnsburg's economic life is no exception. The preacher continues to praise hard work and upright living; the merchant maintains an entrepreneurial instinct and an orientation to the international market. As in the olden days, when only a concerted effort could control the sea, Rijnsburg's leaders of church and commerce preach harmony and collaboration.

Economic Recovery

Most of Holland is no longer as religious-minded as Rijnsburg, but the same traditional values abide throughout the country. Compared with people in other countries, the Dutch are productive, enterprising, and not particularly prone to strikes. Their economy is well planned and strongly focused on the international market. Immediately following the war, however, rapid population growth placed great strain on the nation's economy. In 1900 Holland's population numbered only 5 million inhabitants. By 1950 this number had doubled to 10 million. In 1990, the Dutch population was recorded at 15 million people. An acute housing shortage forced many large families to move into very small living spaces. Food was scarce and basic luxuries, like cars or short vacations, were undreamed of. In this difficult postwar period 500,000 Dutch people, in search of better living conditions, chose, with their government's encouragement, to emigrate to Canada, Australia, New Zealand, the United States, and other countries.

Many young people suffered under the dreariness of life in postwar Holland. The novel *The Evenings* (1947), by Gerard Kornelis van het Reve, could not paint a more convincing picture of one young man's depression during this time. The book describes ten evenings in the life of Frits van Egters. Frits is fed up with life in the office where he works and feels that only his evenings are "real life." Frits tries to close the gap he feels between himself and others, but he never succeeds. His life instead remains filled only with frustration, sick jokes, and boredom. His hidden homosexual feelings are only part of the problem. The larger issue is the lack of any goal in his life. There are no illusions left in the world Frits lives in. *The Evenings*, a hallmark of postwar Dutch literature, realistically portrays the experiences of people during this transitional period in Dutch history.

Cooperation

For postwar Holland to ensure its people a livable existence, it had to accelerate its transition from an agricultural to an industrial society. The

U.S. Marshall Plan—granting 1.1 billion dollars to Holland alone—provided a sound base for reaching that goal. But much more was needed. The Dutch had to carry out this immense task themselves. Propaganda campaigns were initiated to spark people's interest and motivation. One such effort in 1951, supported by the Ministry of Economic Affairs and two Dutch broadcasting companies, invited young adults to write essays on the industrial future of Holland. One entrant named Kees Rijnvos, a young man from the *polder* village of Standdaarbuiten, felt that his life was dismal and, like so many other teens, he was dissatisfied with his home. His daily main meal was potatoes and gravy; his house was cramped and small. While writing his essay, he reported, he was surrounded by his parents, seven brothers, and two sisters, all playing cards in the same room. But beyond his day-to-day life, Kees's essay touched on a theme current in Holland at that time: a belief in progress.

Kees was selected as one of the twelve contest winners and, along with the eleven others, was awarded a nationwide tour of progressive Dutch companies. He was able to experience some other exciting innovations: a night in a hotel, a telephone beside his bed, a pack of cigarettes on the nightstand.

Four decades later, Kees is a professor of Economics and Rector at the Erasmus University of Rotterdam. Looking back in a newspaper interview, he was able to recall his family's own "progress": In 1949 came the first radio; in 1953 a flush toilet was installed, followed by a refrigerator and the first family vacation in 1959; in 1961 the Rijnvos family bought a small car and in 1967 a TV set. That timetable was generally the same for most families throughout Holland.

Although the Dutch were as divided as ever on political and religious issues, these differences were never allowed to hold back economic progress. On the contrary, cooperation was fundamental to a joint effort at making life better "for us all." Workers accepted a wage freeze for many years. Cooperation among employers, trade unions, and the government was coordinated under a newly established system whereby policies were, and still are, determined through discussion.

Export

As Holland recovered and even prospered, it outgrew its old ways. With only a small internal market, industrial expansion had to be sought abroad. Inevitably, Germany was the first to be involved in that expansion. As one Dutch politician put it: "The Netherlands won't make it if there's no prosperity in Germany." Cooperation with the Germans met surprisingly little resistance. The Dutch willingness to put hostilities aside in favor of trade had survived the war. Holland's economic expansion increased in the 1950's, involving ever larger international circles. In 1957 the European Economic Community (EEC) was founded. Six Western European countries, including Holland, agreed to create a common market inside which many existing trade barriers were lifted. This greatly facilitated the export of Dutch agricultural and industrial products to other member states. By 1989, total Dutch exports had mounted to 228 billion guilders (120 billion dollars), which puts it in ninth place on the list of the world's biggest exporting countries. In total, Dutch exports account for about 60 percent of the national income.

Dutch trucking, which has always operated internationally, carries one quarter of all European cargo traffic. Huig de Groot's ideal of free trade among all countries has been realized within Europe. Under less hostile conditions than existed three centuries before, Holland was able to reestablish itself as the European carrier of bulk goods.

Spurred by exports, the Dutch economy has grown steadily since

Dutch trucking carries one quarter of all European cargo traffic.   Photo by Rijkswaterstaat

World War II. Although the fishing and shipbuilding industries play only a modest role in today's economy, there is still money to be made from the sea. Dutch tugboats and Dutch dredging companies are, in their respective fields, still world leaders.

On a national scale, however, port activities are of much greater importance. Thirty percent of all goods transported by sea and loaded or unloaded in the European Community (as the expanded version of the EEC is now called) pass through Dutch ports. Some 40 percent of all European inland carrying trade is in the hands of Dutch shippers.

The World's Busiest Port

The largest share of these activities is centered in Rotterdam. The city of Rotterdam shows, on a larger and more contemporary scale than Rijnsburg, the dynamic side of Dutch economy. As the Dutch say, the people of Rotterdam are always prepared to "roll their sleeves up for work." The club song of Rotterdam's soccer team, Feyenoord, entitled *"Geen woorden maar daden"* ("Actions speak louder than words"), sums up the city's mentality.

Europoort Rotterdam: more than one million transport containers per year. Photo courtesy of Europe Comined Terminals

Rotterdam is located between the North Sea, the busiest sea route in the world, and the densely populated western European continent. Rotterdam is also the main gateway of a vast waterway network that stretches across Europe.

Rotterdam's port comprises two separate ports. Within the city limits there is the old port, frequented every year by thousands of sea cargo ships and tens of thousands of inland waterway vessels. A second port has been created outside the city. Europoort, as it is called, is accessible to the supertankers, roll-on/roll-off (ro-ro) ships, and container ships that dominate modern sea traffic. Measured by surface, capacity, and volume of trade, this twofold Rotterdam port is the biggest in the world, handling almost double the tonnage of New York, now rated fourth in the world (behind Singapore and Kobe).

Industry and Agriculture

Industrial companies are still the indispensable cornerstone of the Dutch economy. Some forty of them, partially or completely under Dutch ownership, have divisions in more than two countries. Among these multinational companies are Royal Shell, Unilever, Philips, Akzo Group (fibers and chemicals), Fokker (aircraft), Heineken (beer), and the new bank ABN/AMRO, the result of a merger between Algemene Bank Nederland (ABN) and Amsterdam-Rotterdam Bank (AMRO).

In the past, industry and agriculture had always been two entirely separate worlds. Industry was the world of smokestacks and assembly lines, agriculture the world of the farmer and nature. Nowhere has this difference become less true than in Holland. Dutch farms have become small factories in themselves. Machines are now used to milk all Dutch cows, but even this will be changing. These machines still need to be operated by people. New milking robots can milk cows five times a day

The Big Three

As substantial employers, investors, and taxpayers in the Netherlands, industrial companies are vital to the Dutch economy. Their elaborate research and development programs are likewise responsible for much of the technological innovation in Holland.

The leading three companies in Holland are Royal Shell, Unilever, and Philips, ranked respectively as the second, twentieth, and twenty-second of the world's largest industrial companies.

The Dutch branch of Royal Shell, called "The Royal," began

The Dutch gold mine: Natural gas plant in the province of Groningen. Photo from Cas Oorthuys archive

operations in 1890 with the possession of an oilfield in the East Dutch Indies. In 1907 "The Royal" merged with the British oil transportation company Shell, obtaining a 60 percent interest in the group, leaving Shell with an interest of 40 percent.

Worldwide, the present Royal Shell Group maintains its key role in the production and transportation of oil products and chemicals. Together with Exxon, Royal Shell exploits Holland's most precious mineral: natural gas. Natural gas today accounts for 7.5 percent of the Dutch national income.

Unilever is a combined Dutch-British enterprise, the result of a merger in 1930 between Jurgens & Van den Bergh (Holland) and Lever Brothers (England). Unilever is one of the world's leading producers of foodstuffs, detergents and toiletries, and is also involved with chemical products, cattle fodder, fisheries, and transportation. It runs five hundred companies in seventy-five countries.

Philips Electronics is the most Dutch of the big three. Its old name—Philips Gloeilampenfabriek (Philips Light Bulb Factory)—points to the early roots of the company's success. Philips still makes light bulbs, but the manufacture of radio, TV, CD, and video equipment, in addition to an endless variety of domestic appliances, has become the company's chief enterprise. International operations have been established in sixty countries. Philips's NatLab (Physics Laboratory) in Eindhoven is the largest industrial laboratory in Europe. In its research and development of new technology, Philips participates in joint ventures with corporations like AT&T, Matsushita, Du Pont, and Siemens.

while the farmer is in bed or doing something else. The robot knows when to start; it works in synchronization with the cow's milk-producing cycles.

Holland's 93 million chickens are also watched by machines—automation enables one person to oversee ten thousand chickens—as are the country's 14 million pigs. Up to six thousand fattening hogs, out of Holland's 14 million pigs, can be supervised by one person.

Highly mechanized pig farm in the province of North Brabant.   Photo by Theo van Stegeren

Agricultural automation has introduced great improvements in farm productivity. Dutch farms are generally regarded as the world's most efficient and productive. Holland's moderate, humid climate and fertile soil furnish a highly suitable environment for agriculture. The cultivation of vegetables and ornamental plants has been dramatically improved. Automation and computers also play a central role in horticulture. Greenhouses for growing tomatoes, cucumbers, and other vegetables resemble laboratories. Temperature and humidity are computer monitored. Small sprinklers automatically provide plants with the nutrients they need. Even the soil in which the plants are rooted has been adapted. Today a synthetic material called "rock wool," which requires no toxic chemicals, is used instead of earth.

The Westland region in South Holland, known as "the city of glass." Lettuce, tomatoes, grapes, and bell peppers are grown here in highly computerized greenhouses. Energy is in part provided by windmills. Photo by Rijkswaterstaat

To Spend or to Save

Most Dutch people earn enough money to enjoy the fruits of their country's expanding economy. The Dutch, however, are not big spenders by nature. They are reluctant to spend a lot on goods and services. As one observer remarked, the Dutch export excellent butter but they cover their own slice of bread with margarine. Luxury is still a somewhat embarrassing matter in Holland. People do their best to earn more for themselves, but according to public opinion, that wealth is of less importance than the community's overall prosperity. This attitude helps to explain why the Dutch do not mind paying up to 60 percent of their income in taxes and why the percentage of Holland's national product allocated to social services is the highest in Europe.

For the Dutch saving and investing are attractive alternatives to spending money. Almost all Dutch people entrust a considerable share of their income to banks, investment funds, pension funds, and insurance companies. These treasurers of Holland's wealth are not afraid to search abroad for the most profitable investments, making Holland, after Japan, the world's leading investor in foreign real estate.

The Dutch also invest in foreign industries, particularly in the United States. With the United Kingdom at the top, the Netherlands is the second largest investor in American companies. Americans do not mind that much, since economic traffic between the United States and Holland flows in both directions. The Americans are the largest foreign investors in the Netherlands and enjoy a larger trade surplus with the Netherlands than with any other country.

The economic success of the Dutch can be tied to the country's work ethic. Netherlanders start working at an early age. From age thirteen, more than half of the children find work after school. Boys earn money with paper routes, repair, or gardening jobs. Girls baby-sit or work in offices and restaurants. Parents generally don't force this on their children. Dutch teens choose their own jobs and keep the money for themselves. Once out of high school, young people often continue to earn extra money, even if they have regular jobs during the day.

In general, the Dutch are content with the prosperity their economy is able to produce. Eight out of ten Dutch people feel almost or completely satisfied with their incomes. An even higher percentage feel their own families live prosperously. Despite their rosy circumstances, however, the Dutch would not like to be portrayed as materialists. When asked what is most important in their lives, only two percent of Dutch people mention a high salary as the most important thing in life. A happy marriage comes second, but almost unanimously, good health comes in first place.

CHAPTER VIII

Double Democracy

Holland is a full-fledged democracy with publicly elected representatives, a free press, and independent judges. Political power is distributed among various governmental units at the national, provincial, and municipal levels. These units are the parliament, the provincial assemblies, and the city councils, each with their own budget and areas of responsibility. On the bottom rung of the democratic ladder are the *waterschappen* (water control boards).

The Hague is the center of Dutch politics, where executive government, parliament, and civil service offices and meeting halls are located. All actions taken by the executive branch must be approved by the Dutch parliament, still officially called the States General. Parliament has two houses, with 75 members in the Upper House and 150 in the

The many different posters reflect the variety of Dutch political parties.   Photo by ANP.

Lower House. The members of the Lower House are elected by popular vote, members of the Upper House by the popularly elected provincial assemblies. All laws have to pass both the Upper and Lower Houses. The attention of the public and press is usually focused on the Lower House, which meets more frequently and has greater power than the Upper House. It has, for instance, the right to amend legislation proposed by the executive branch and to initiate legislation itself, whereas the Upper House only has the power to veto proposals from the Lower House.

Ministers and members of the two Houses are drawn from among the three leading parties and five or six smaller ones. No single political party has ever managed to gain an absolute majority in Holland. The government has always consisted of a coalition of two or more parties, ensuring that at least two important political currents share responsibility for the government's policies. The main parties are the *Christen Democratisch Appèl* (Christian Democratic Alliance), the *Partij van de Arbeid* (Labor Party), the conservative-liberal party *VVD* (People's Party for Freedom and Democracy), and the progressive-liberal party D 66 (Democrats 1966).

The diversity of small-scale political parties in Holland is remarkable. Three small orthodox Christian parties, the *Gereformeerd Politiek Verbond* (Reformed Political Union), the *Staatkundig Gereformeerde Partij* (Political Reformed Party), and the *Reformatorisch Politieke Federatie* (Christian-Reformed Political Federation), base their politics directly on the Bible. The Political Reformed Party, for instance, opposes the continuing secularization of society and the vote for women. In parliament these parties sometimes cooperate with the leading Christian party, the Christian Democratic Alliance, but what separates them is their radical resistance to accepting compromise in carrying out their principles.

While until recently a recognized small official group, the Communists no longer function as a separate political party. In 1989 they formed a union with three other small left-wing groups.

Kings and Queens

Holland's King or Queen has a special role in the political process. Laws require the monarchs signature before they go into effect, but ministers—not monarchs—are responsible for each action taken by government. When a law is passed and later judged to be in error, criticism is always directed against the minister concerned or the party in power when it was enacted. If a monarch refuses to countersign a law, which happens very rarely, the minister's opinion prevails. According to law, the monarch cannot be forced to go along with that opinion. In that case, however, the monarch would have to fire the appropriate minister. Up to now that situation has never occurred, since it is in no one's interest for conflicts to reach such an extreme stage.

The constitution states that the reigning monarch is prohibited from engaging in politics. Ministers are in turn accountable for the King's or Queen's actions. The monarch's speeches are read in advance by at least one minister. Were something to be said for which no minister was willing to claim responsibility, the appropriate minister or the coalition in power would have to resign. But if this imaginary situation should ever occur, there would also be another possibility: The constitution provides for a complex procedure that allows the States General to decide that the monarch is incompetent to reign.

Many of the monarch's official activities are ceremonial: He or she receives foreign heads of state, ennobles worthy individuals, and grants pardons. For the present Queen, Beatrix, these activities are only half of the job. She enjoys posing critical questions and advising decision-makers in the areas of politics, science, welfare, developmental aid to Third World countries, and the arts. Whatever she asks or advises remains confidential. Only on appropriate occasions, such as her annual Christmas speech, may she express her own opinions more openly. In such cases she likes to call attention to topics like social injustice and environmental health.

Elections and Coalitions

Everyone in Holland is entitled to establish new political parties and to participate in elections, as long as the aims of the parties are not

Monarchy

The Dutch monarchy is officially linked to the House of Orange. In the words of Article 24 of the constitution: "The title to the Throne shall be hereditary and shall be vested in the legitimate descendants of King William I, Prince of Orange Nassau."

The King or Queen is not elected by the people or parliament, but inherits the throne by birth. Although inheritance of power does not seem to fit in a modern democracy, the monarchy finds overwhelming support among the Dutch people.

Queen Wilhelmina reigned from 1898 till 1948, when she abdicated in favor of her daughter Juliana. In 1980 Juliana in her turn transferred royal power to her eldest daughter, Beatrix, the present monarch of the Netherlands.

Queen Beatrix, Prince Claus, and their three sons. Photo by ANP

contrary to law. There is no minimum share of the vote required. Only one obstacle has to be overcome: A new party must deposit 250 guilders (130 dollars) if it wishes to compete locally, or 18,000 guilders (9,500 dollars) if it wishes to compete in the elections for the national parliament.

At the local level, political diversity is greatest. Eight hundred "one-person parties" participate in city-council meetings. These parties are founded by individual men and women who feel the leading parties have overlooked their particular interests.

In all elections, whether for national parliament, provincial assemblies, or municipality councils, a system of proportional representation is used. This means that the distribution of seats in parliament or council among the parties corresponds as closely as possible with the distribution of votes. A party obtaining 10 percent of the vote cast also obtains 10 percent—or as near as possible to 10 percent—of the seats. In the United States, by contrast, a party winning 49 percent of the vote in a district might not be represented at all.

Elections for the national parliament are held every four years. Following an election, the Queen or King becomes directly involved in the question of which parties should try to form a government together. She or he invites political-party representatives to the palace and weighs their opinions carefully. Again, the Queen's or King's consultations are kept confidential, but it is not a secret that they usually result in a proposal that the monarch approves of. Some critics argue that this gives an unelected person too large a role and for that reason does not belong in a modern democracy. But since the monarch applies his or her power with prudence and because it is his or her only activity of a political nature, few people object.

After the consultations, the Queen or King appoints an *informateur*, a politician who investigates, on behalf of the crown, whether a proposed cabinet will succeed. In a parliamentary system of government, cabinets are made up of representatives from a variety of parties that together hold a majority of seats in the legislature. In the United States, a cabinet is formed by the President and is not necessarily related to the makeup of Congress. Once the *informateur* has completed this task, which may take several weeks or even months, he or she returns to the royal palace with a judgment on the matter. Of course the biggest parties are most likely to enter the coalition. The Catholic People's Party, which merged in 1973 with Abraham Kuyper's Anti-Revolutionary Party and a third Christian party to become the new *Christen Democratisch Appèl,* (Christian Democratic Alliance), has continuously been on center stage for the last half century, participating without interruption in all government coalitions. Coalitions are alternately formed with the *Partij van de Arbeid* (Labor Party) and the two major liberal parties, *VVD* (People's Party for Freedom and Democracy) and *D 66* (Democrats 1966).

After receiving the *informateur*'s advice, the Queen or King appoints a *formateur*, who is charged with forming the new government. Under his or her guidance the parties that are going to form the government negotiate about the division of ministerial posts. The biggest parties claim the largest number of posts and try to carry off the most important ones, such as Secretary of the Treasury and Secretary of the Department of Economics. During the same negotiations, the coalition parties reach an agreement that sketches in broad outlines the plans of the new government for the next four years. This essential moment in Dutch democracy takes place behind closed doors. The opposition—the parties that don't participate in the government—have to wait for the results. The more arrangements the coalition parties lay down at this stage, the less there remains to be discussed and changed in the public sessions of Lower House and Upper House later on. Once the negotiations have been ended successfully, the new government is sworn in at the royal palace.

Now the process of attempting to win and hold the consent of parliament begins. Often a government succeeds in serving out its four-year term. But if, as has happened from time to time, a majority of parliament disagrees fundamentally with the coalition's politics, it may withdraw its consent. The "government falls" and new elections are necessary.

To Vote or Not to Vote

How alive is Dutch democracy? Practically all Netherlanders favor the system of parliament and provincial and municipality councils. A majority—on average 60 percent of the enfranchised citizens—takes the trouble of going to a polling place on an average election day. Voters select an individual candidate, but in doing so they also support a party list, or slate. Seats are apportioned on the basis of the percentage of the vote each party gets; so when the election returns are counted, the party knows how many seats it is getting and divides them among the candidates on the slate based on votes for the individual candidates.

Behind the 60 percent that vote one sees a different picture. Only 4 percent of the population are active members of political parties, and of these people only one tenth—that is, approximately .4 percent of all Dutch voters—participate in deciding who will be a candidate for parliament and what will be on the party's political platform. While a higher percentage of Americans participates in nominating candidates by voting in primaries, the diversity of Dutch parties makes it easier to get a candidate on a local ballot.

There are several reasons for this low rate of participation. Some people are simply not interested in politics. They may blame the Dutch politicians who, in their opinion, are interested in the voter's opinions only during election time and focus their attention on their own careers as soon as the elections are over. As one worker from Amsterdam said in a newspaper interview:

I still vote on election day. But if you would ask me: Do you know for whom? I must say no. I simply put my cross on the ballot. It really doesn't matter. After all they don't do anything for me. They promise a lot, but once they are elected and have a limousine with a driver they forget about it.

Another explanation for the low degree of political participation is that many people, instead of becoming members of a party or contacting a politician, prefer other ways of making their influence felt. Practically all Netherlanders are members of or contributors to clubs, associations, and foundations in which professionals as well as voluntary workers pursue ecological, religious, or social aims. These networks control, scrutinize, and criticize every aspect of life, politics not excluded.

Verzuiling

This involvement in voluntary organizations is in part a heritage of the *verzuiling* of Dutch society that arose during the nineteenth century. A *zuil* is a column or pillar. *Verzuiling* (pillarization) referred to the way each ideological bloc had created its own isolated "pillar"—a pillar not based upon class, race, or regional background but on a way of thinking and believing. In the nineteenth century, the age of industrialization, Dutch religious and political leaders such as Abraham Kuyper were afraid that some kind of class struggle would divide their own ranks, and consequently they began stressing their own group's inner unity and solidarity. "Keep away from dissenters" was their message. "Limit your contacts to followers of the same faith." Catholics, Protestants, and socialists organized themselves into tightly knit networks, building their own circuits of churches, schools, clubs, social services, hospitals, and shops. In every town Protestants, Roman Catholics, socialists, and liberals lived side by side, often on the same street or in the same neighborhood, without ever talking to each other. At the same time, these pillars together carried the full weight of society. To keep society together, tasks were divided in a pragmatic way: The rank-and-file members of the coexisting movements lived within their faith, while national leaders cooperated with each other.

There were, and are, other places in the world where religious groups led their lives in seclusion. The unique thing about the Dutch situation was that this way of living actually shaped all of society. The various religious groups did not want a society in which everything was left to private initiative, but they did not want the state to have a monopoly on providing care either. And so they created an intermediate layer of organizations and clubs that could bridge the gap between individual citizens and the state. In education, labor, social welfare, and broadcasting these groups would have their say in the administration of the country.

This explains the paradox that is still found in Dutch society: Everyone disagrees with everyone else, yet the political situation remains stable. *Verzuiling* has created a basic "agreement to disagree." Discussion and protest are part of the game, as long as nobody rocks the boat too much. Although the various ideological blocs tend to regard each other with suspicion, this rarely turns into hostility. This peaceful coexistence persisted until well into the second half of this century. Even in the 1960's, Roman Catholic boys and girls started their careers at Roman Catholic primary schools and continued at Roman Catholic high schools and universities. For their leisure activities they were bound to become members of a Roman Catholic soccer club or scouting organization. At home information was drawn from Roman Catholic newspapers and a Roman Catholic broadcasting company. Their fathers worked for Roman Catholic bosses, and their mothers did their shopping exclusively with Roman Catholic butchers and grocers. Marriage, of course, was within the faith.

Action Groups

With the declining power of church and its beliefs, this pattern began to fade. In the 1960's and 1970's the old barriers melted away. A younger generation felt imprisoned by *verzuiling*. New political parties arose in response to the general feeling of discontent—among them a liberal-democratic, a socialist-democratic, and a left-radical party. New laws allowed students and workers to have their say in universities, high schools, communities, companies, hospitals, and even the army and prisons.

Since the 1960's thousands of *aktiegroepen* (action groups) have been founded by citizens. They usually rally around one issue. That issue may be of interest for the whole country: the lack of safety in automobile traffic, for instance. But smaller cases arise as well. Someone may go to the local newspaper and tell them that he or she has started a movement to promote local automobile safety, and a new action group is born. Groups organize petitions, meetings, and strikes. International comparative studies show that the desire to protest is exceptionally high in Holland.

Ministries and municipalities spend much of their time and money in consulting with these groups. Some action groups are actually sponsored by the government. The municipality of Rotterdam, for instance, pays more than 1 million guilders (well over 500,000 dollars) a year to citizens' groups involved in city renovation plans. With this money they can hire their own advisers, produce their own community newspapers, and become better partners for discussions with city politicians and civil servants.

Some groups have even turned to violence. One minority ethnic group, the South Moluccans from Indonesia, organized several spectacular hijackings. The South Moluccans blamed Holland for letting Indonesia take control of their home country. The hijackings—first of a train and the Indonesian consulate, later of another train and a primary school—were a complete shock to the Dutch population. In these actions, intended to force the recognition of an independent Moluccan Republic in Indonesia, several people were killed.

Between 1975 and 1985, a new series of violent confrontations followed. Squatters protested against real-estate speculation in the big cities, which was intensifying the housing shortage and pushing rents higher. Armed with sticks, bricks, and slingshots, squatters engaged in battles with police forces. Hundreds of people were wounded. Several times local police were assisted by a specially trained paramilitary police force, called *Mobiele Eenheid* (Mobile Unit). This *Mobiele Eenheid* is equipped with helmets, shields, tear gas, and armored cars.

Serious as these confrontations may have been, they have not led to an enduring extremism. In the end, the Dutch are too sober-minded to engage in drawn-out bloody fights for long or to start a revolution. Their need for consensus is too strong. They would rather resolve their conflicts through meetings and compromise. Civil and police authorities have gone to great lengths to employ weapons that are effective but harmless. Their opponents have likewise never resorted to extended terrorist campaigns, as has happened elsewhere around the world.

Protest and Harmony

To maintain harmony, protest in Holland often contains a *ludieke* (playful) element. One of the first *ludieke* actions in Holland even managed to catch the world's attention. In 1966 young activists, calling themselves "Provos" (derived from the word "provoke"), declared themselves against the marriage of Queen Beatrix and the German Claus von Amsberg. One activist threw a bomb at the golden coach in which the Queen was being carried to her wedding ceremony. After the smoke had lifted, it was apparent that it had only been a smoke bomb. No one had been hurt. Most people were shocked by the action, but the protesters and their sympathizers were proud: They had made their protest public in an effective yet largely harmless way.

Actions like these show the traditional Dutch aversion to authority. This was again proved in 1985 during the Pope John Paul II's visit to

Police unit clears an illegally occupied house. To ease the atmosphere and prevent the squatters from aggression, two policemen masquerade as Sinterklaas and Black Pete. Note the shield and walkie-talkie. Photo by Bert Verhoeff

Holland. His advisers had expected this trip to be the "most difficult" of all his visits abroad. They proved to be right. Even before the Pontiff had taken his first step on Dutch soil, a television company had aired a series parodying the Pope's upcoming tour through Holland. During the visit itself the Pope was confronted with demonstrators, empty streets, and trick questions. Those making life difficult for the Pope were largely liberal Dutch Catholics and atheists, not Protestants. When the Pope's visit was over, Prime Minister Lubbers—himself a Catholic—did not condemn the protest. "The mere fact that Rome tells us Dutchmen something is enough for us to respond negatively," he said.

Fighting between police and demonstrators during visit of Pope John Paul II in 1985.
Photo by ANP

Political protest in Holland has stimulated Dutch creativity. NATO marching bands have slipped on marbles scattered by antimilitary demonstrators. Ministers have had buckets of paint poured over their heads, and one minister has found his front yard dug up by protesting youngsters. Another form of protest, the mass demonstration, may take on a half-serious, half-festive atmosphere. People paint their faces and sing songs; bands provide a cheerful note.

The advantages of creative forms of protest are obvious. Their originality attracts the attention of the media, the public, and the politicians. A seemingly innocent protest is not so easily cleared away by police. Were the police to intervene, demonstrators would seem the underdogs in public opinion, and the police would be accused of unnecessary force. Finally, if you do have to spend your precious free time at a protest, why not have a good time as well?

The government tries to take everyone's interests into account by listening to a host of advisory boards in which the public is represented by experts. Action groups outside the parliament are not easily disregarded either. They may voice their opinions in special hearings. The government recognizes that new problems may be brought to light in these hearings and that insights into the possible effects of a new policy can be gained. By trial and error, Dutch government has learned to cope with the double democracy of parliamentary and extraparliamentary activities.

Welfare and Justice

The Dutch state is a welfare state, the result of a lengthy social struggle in which trade unions and the Labor Party played an important role. Willem Drees is generally recognized as the architect of the modern Dutch welfare state. The socialist Drees presided over four consecutive cabinets between 1948 and 1958. During this decade the foundation of the new welfare system was laid with the introduction and revision of, for instance, the Old Age Pensions Act and the Unemployment Act. The welfare state is built upon laws and rules that guarantee citizens a decent existence. In many respects that guarantee is fulfilled. There are no slums, nobody dies of hunger or poverty, and very few people are homeless. There is a minimum wage for the employed and a minimum income for all adult citizens. A network of doctors, dentists, and hospitals is in place, and practically everyone has public or private health insurance, which allows them to make use of these facilities. If people are sick or unemployed, they may obtain subsidies not far short of the wage they would normally earn. A so-called "social" approach to housing has indeed provided "decent" dwellings for 90 percent of the population. People's health, education, and well-being are largely provided for by the government.

Spending by the Central Government

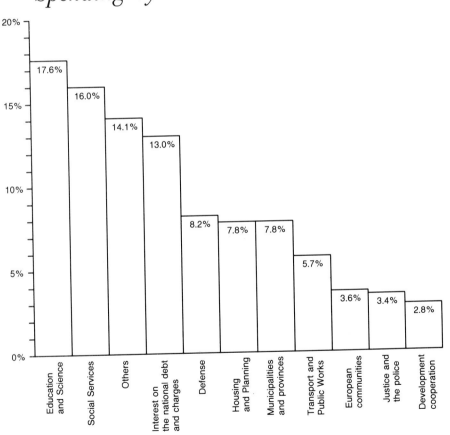

Guaranteeing a decent existence for every citizen of the Netherlands is an expensive undertaking. Almost one third of the country's gross national product is spent on social services, with many more billions of dollars allocated to housing and health care. Employers and citizens pay for the system, partly in the form of taxes, partly in the form of federal insurance premiums. After the Scandinavian countries, Holland has the world's heaviest tax burden.

Taxes and premiums are collected under a "progressive" system of taxation. People with the lowest income pay approximately 35 percent of their wages in taxes. The rich are taxed much more heavily; up to 60 percent of their income goes to taxes. The progressive tax system diminishes differences in income level. Several years ago one Dutch Prime Minister remarked that his country possessed both the richest poor and the poorest rich people in the world. There is still some truth to that statement.

The Welfare System

The extent of the Dutch welfare system is only comparable with that of Scandinavian countries. In 1987 approximately 3.5 million people received a public allowance, benefit, or pension. In that year a total sum of 128 billion guilders (67 billion dollars) was allocated for orphans, widows, poor, disabled, unemployed, retired, and other people in need of assistance.

Two kinds of benefits exist. The first is available only for employees; the second applies to the general population. A safety net has also been placed beneath these benefits, called the *Algemene Bijstandswet* (General Assistance Act).

A stroll down a typical Dutch street might show how citizens use the system in many different ways.

The Desire for a Middle Way

The Dutch pursuit of social equality is firmly rooted in its society. People do not want the gap between rich and poor to grow wider. On the contrary, research indicates that more than half believe the difference should be reduced. The Dutch like their prosperity, but only so long as extremes in wealth and poverty are avoided.

OPINION CONCERNING THE LEVELING OF INCOME 1970–1987
(IN PERCENTAGES)

	1970	1980	1987
a. The differences between high and low incomes should be:			
made much larger	1	2	2
made somewhat larger	3	3	10
kept as is	28	19	27
made somewhat smaller	34	40	35
made much smaller	33	36	26
b. Class differences should be smaller than they are now:			
strongly agree	25	15	14
agree	44	56	49
(strongly) disagree	14	15	17
no opinion	18	14	20

In the first house on the street, No. 1, resides a retired couple. The man was formerly a civil servant but now receives a small pension from the government as his former employer. That pension is not substantial enough, however, to meet the minimum income level guaranteed for all adult citizens by the Dutch state. For that reason he and his wife receive an additional monthly pension provided by the General Old Age Pension Act (AOW). The amount will not make the man and woman rich, but it will be the bare minimum they need in a modern Western society.

In the house next door, at No. 3, lives a woman with two small children. The woman is divorced. She is raising her children independently and does some volunteer work in the evening hours. The only income she has is her alimony, not nearly enough to support herself, her children, and her two cats. To bridge this gap, she receives an additional benefit from the General Assistance Act. This act is the keystone of the Dutch welfare system, entitling every Dutch citizen over age eighteen to a minimum level of benefits. The act is designed to catch people who, for whatever reason, fall by the wayside within the regular welfare system. The General Assistance Act provides benefits that will bring the woman at No. 3 to the same minimum level as her neighbors.

But even with these benefits, she will not be able to afford her rent. The state has therefore provided a solution for that problem as well. Dutch law states that tenants in Holland can be expected to spend a reasonable share of their income on rent, but they are entitled to receive a subsidy when that percentage becomes too high. The woman accordingly applies for help and receives an individual grant.

On the opposite side of the street, in a row of one-family houses, lives a more well-to-do family. The man earns a reasonable income, enough to enable him and his wife, their three children, and the dog to go on holidays twice a year: in the summer to the sunny beaches of Spain, in the winter to the snowy mountains of Austria. The oldest daughter, however, has just begun her studies at the university. The costs of college fees, books, and traveling exceed the capabilities of even this middle-class family. The daughter therefore applies for a government loan. These loans are granted automatically to every student between eighteen and thirty years old and consist of a fixed sum intended as a financial base. This sum will be paid back to the state much later, but without interest. If the grant is insufficient to cover costs, supplementary scholarships and interest-bearing loans are available.

The Dutch welfare system provides people with more than just money; it provides them with independence as well. Young people get the opportunity to stand on their own feet from the age of eighteen or nineteen on. Women do not have to marry for purely financial reasons. Retired people are able to wait longer before appealing to their children or grandchildren for money or housing. The sense of independence that results colors the feelings of the Dutch people and, consequently, influences the society as a whole.

Black Money

The Dutch attitude toward the welfare system is perplexing. Although complaints about the tax burden are frequently heard, proposals to cut social expenditures are unpopular. The Netherlands has always been a pioneer in welfare. By the seventeenth century many Dutch cities possessed charity houses, where orphans, the old, and the poor could find shelter, food, and care. That tradition continues. Today the abolition or serious reduction of the welfare system is out of the question. The Dutch are proud of their system. One citizen remarked: "Sometimes we may put down the welfare system and complain that payments should be higher or lower. But we must have it all the same! If I'm hit by a

streetcar tomorrow, my family won't find their security destroyed over-
night."

Holland's situation sounds ideal, but it is not. Compared to the degree
of poverty in neighboring countries like Great Britain and France,
Holland does reasonably well. But by the country's own standards,
poverty does exist. Ten percent of the Dutch population lives in inade-
quate housing, is not well educated, and is offered few job opportunities.
Because the poor in Holland tend to isolate themselves from others, this
poverty is not so readily visible.

Once people fall below the poverty line, contact with others is quickly
lost. The tragic thing is that the allowance that helps them survive

Young tramps spending the night in an empty railroad car.   Photo by Bert Verhoeff

simultaneously enhances their helplessness. Someone receiving welfare from the General Assistance Act, for instance, is not allowed to study or take a part-time job. Meeting other people and learning new skills becomes more difficult. Like patients who stay for a long time in a hospital, they grow accustomed to their dependence on the state and lose their own initiative.

An additional problem is a loss of personal privacy. Those receiving an allowance from the General Assistance Act are required to report every six months to a civil servant of the welfare department to show their passport, residence permit, unemployment record, housing agreement, rent subsidy papers, National Health Service card, bank deposit book, and financial statements. They are asked detailed questions about their private lives. Authorities believe this kind of monitoring is necessary to prevent abuse of the costly facilities. But for those honestly seeking help, it can be a humiliating and discouraging experience.

More money would be needed to improve the situation of the Dutch lower class. Taxpayers, however, do not seem very cooperative in that respect. Despite feelings of pride and solidarity, millions of Netherlanders use illegal methods to relieve their private tax burden. They participate in the "black," or shadow, economy, where no taxes are paid. Plumbers, electricians, waiters, hairdressers, auto mechanics, painters, and gardeners "working black"—what we would call working "off the books"—provide their services to almost every Dutch household and avoid paying taxes on their incomes. Youngsters often fail to report their small earnings. People with regular jobs may provide themselves with extra money by restoring houses or giving driving lessons in the evening hours. None of this is reported to the government. Others "forget" to buy a ticket on the streetcar, pay no income tax on the salary of their housemaid, or buy their furniture and cars on the black market. That people are depriving the government of the billions of guilders it desper-

A streetcar in Amsterdam. Its nickname is the "black passenger tram," referring to the fact that many passengers travel "black"—illegally or illicitly, in this case without paying the fare. Photo by Theo van Stegeren

ately needs to keep the welfare system going does not appear to be a concern.

In 1985 a governmental committee estimated that state losses related to black market activities amounted to approximately 19 billion guilders (10 billion dollars) a year, equivalent to about 12 percent of the annual budget. If one is looking for reasons why the Dutch government has difficulty maintaining the social welfare system, the black market is one.

No Ghettos

Public housing is another feature of the Dutch welfare system. In the Netherlands, good housing is considered extremely important for society as a whole. Public health, educational advancement, and opportunities for work and prosperity are all promoted when good housing is amply available for everyone. To avoid class barriers and ghetto-ization, authorities plan suburbs and neighborhoods with houses for people of all income levels. In an attempt to keep housing rents low, the central government awards grants to housing associations responsible for building projects. These grants in turn lead to lower rents for the eventual tenants.

The post–World War II population boom sparked an acute shortage of housing in the Netherlands. Initially, the construction of large-scale satellite cities and suburbs was tried as a solution to the housing situation. Villages were renamed as so-called *groeisteden* (overflow towns). Endless rows of apartment blocks were thrown together, many of inferior quality.

Public housing project in Amsterdam.   Photo by Theo van Stegeren

It gradually became clear that inhabitants of these housing projects were unhappy with their new living conditions. The apartments were too impersonal and uniform. Crime and vandalism flourished. Those who could afford to moved to better areas, leaving the poor behind. In spite of all good intentions, slums were taking shape.

As a result, a more humane way of building was chosen. New residential areas were developed, filled with rows of imaginatively designed and playfully positioned houses, trees, and shrubbery. This type of environment was better suited to people's needs.

While cities and towns expanded rapidly onto surrounding fields and grasslands, many older urban areas were becoming run-down. Houses and their inhabitants were being swept away to build highways and other large-scale developments. To prevent the appearance of new slums, urban renewal projects were undertaken. Old houses and warehouses were restored; sidewalks were transformed into small squares with jungle gyms, slides, and skateboard slopes for children. To guarantee children's safety, speed bumps were built into streets to reduce the speed of passing automobiles.

These urban renewal areas are no wonders of architectural design. Architects' and contractors' budgets were cut wherever possible. But these projects have at least prevented the general decay of inner cities. Moreover, they have provided people of lower and middle income levels with reasonable housing in the inner cities.

In its attempts to organize a welfare state, the government has increasingly turned itself into the center around which the rest of society revolves. Between 1960 and 1969 approximately one thousand new or revised laws were introduced. That number has now risen to twelve hundred a year. In one interview a speaker for the welfare, public health, and culture departments may announce decisions regarding compensation for test tube fertilization by social insurance and the hospitals in which this operation may be performed, financing of blood-sample testing for the AIDS virus, licensing policy planning for general practitioners and physiotherapists, and so on.

The Dutch welfare state has grown so complicated that governmental departments themselves often do not know how to apply new laws and rules. Many citizens—especially from minority ethnic groups—easily lose track in the maze of rules and regulations. They do not know which rule applies to them, they cannot find the right civil servant. Numerous rules and forms exist for poor or jobless people, but the people for whom they are intended are not able to benefit from them.

Politicians now realize that society may no longer be controlled by increasing the volume of laws and rules. New committees have already made proposals to simplify the system.

Prisons

Crime is widespread throughout the Netherlands, which has a higher rate of petty crimes—bike theft, car burglary, and vandalism—than in other European countries. More serious crimes are not as common, although the arrival of heroin has produced a more ruthless and professional Dutch underworld. Possessing a weapon remains uncommon and unaccepted among ordinary citizens.

Whether criminality should be fought with more stringent or more humane measures has always been a point of controversy in Holland. In the sixteenth century Dirck Volckertsz Coornhert was one of the first writers in Europe to call for criminal-law reform. He observed that harsh punishments like flogging and keelhauling did not improve criminals' behavior and, on the contrary, led to greater isolation from society. Coornhert's revolutionary proposal, set forth in his book *Boeventucht* (*Discipline for Villains*, 1587), was to bring criminals together in prisons and put them to work. Work, he reasoned, would teach prisoners to live honestly. Although his proposal was based on an ideal of human dignity, Coornhert was never blind to the economic advantage: Working prisoners brought in money, and idle vagabonds cost money.

Times have changed. A proposal to put prisoners to work may not be as revolutionary these days as it was in the sixteenth century, but Coornhert's idea of improving lawbreakers is still respected. Dutch judges maintain that prison sentences seldom have a positive effect on people's behavior, instead worsening the criminal's situation through isolation from society or contact with other criminals. Dutch judges are consequently reluctant jailors. When at all possible, young people who have come into conflict with the law for the first time are not sent to jail. An "alternative" punishment is sometimes provided. A juvenile shoplifter might be sent back to the shop where the crime was committed to clean the floor and stock merchandise for several days.

Criminal penalties in Holland are relatively light. Sentences are, on average, milder than in other countries. Holland has the lowest percentage of detainees in Europe. The most extreme sentence, the death penalty, has been abolished. The last executions in Holland took place shortly after World War II, when several German collaborators were shot. Today, the Dutch people are divided over whether the death penalty is acceptable. Recent opinion polls have shown that a slight majority of people are in favor of capital punishment. It is unlikely, however, that the Dutch government will change its position.

The prison system in the Netherlands is remarkably humane. The Prison Act in effect today was in part prepared by legislators who, as members of the resistance, had been seized by the Germans and held captive for years in Dutch prisons and work camps. After the war, these legislators were determined to form a more humane prison system. The system they created keeps a sharp eye on the individual's well-being.

Prisoner in his cell.   Photo by ANP

Both the Criminal Code and the Prison Act state that, while the essential nature of the sentence must be upheld, it should be enforced in a manner that prepares the prisoner for his or her return into society.

This goal is reflected in the way Dutch prisons are run. American observers are particularly amazed that each prisoner is provided with his or her own cell. Prisoners are also granted the opportunity to rent a TV set. These luxuries are disputed in Holland. Some refer to Dutch prisons as "hotels." Considering the general shortage of space, some critics suggest that more than one prisoner be placed in a cell. Sharing a cell, however, is considered a violation of human dignity and privacy. The odds of such a change are small.

Security is a number one priority in Dutch prisons. Yet maximum security is pursued only when absolutely necessary. The prison at Scheveningen, for instance, posts armed guards in watchtowers. Most prisons, however, apply stricter measures only in designated areas. Prison wardens consider maximum security undesirable in view of the increased tensions and disciplinary problems it can cause. Less-evident security has an important psychological function for prisoners: The hope of escape makes prisoners feel better, even if an attempt is never made. When that hope is destroyed by harshly restrictive measures, prisoners may resort to violence and hostage taking.

Prisoners may hope to escape, but actual attempts generally fail. Each year about forty attempts are successful, but within twenty-four weeks 96 percent of the fugitives have been seized again. Hiding is not easy in a small and densely populated country like Holland.

The Dutch habit of reserve has an observable effect in the prisons. There is no violence "in the air." Apart from a single exception, guards are unarmed. A spirit of friendship between guards and prisoners is frequent. Prisoners utilize available sports facilities and participate in group activities. Prisoners and staff in some prisons even celebrate the Sinterklaasfeest together.

While critics call this system "idealistic," the Dutch themselves consider their approach "realistic." All sentences in Holland are temporary (even people who are sentenced to life imprisonment are usually pardoned after twenty years). Every prisoner will return to society. What is the point of keeping people in prison for the rest of their lives?

To prepare convicts for this reintegration into society, prisons offer educational courses and vocational training. Illiterate prisoners are given the opportunity to learn to read and write. Offenders with shorter sentences are placed in what are called "half-open" prisons, where weekend leaves and employment within or outside the prison are permitted. Inmates pass through prison gates in the morning to go to work and return in the evening to be put once again behind prison bars. More serious delinquents are placed in so-called "closed" prisons. Only during the last four or five months of their sentences are they allowed to go to "open prisons."

Interestingly, the recidivism rate—the percentage of convicts who relapse into criminal behavior—for Holland is exactly the same as that for the United States, where most prisons enforce more severe regimens. Criminologists consequently suggest that recidivism is affected by factors other than the softness or harshness of prison systems.

Abortion, Euthanasia, Drugs

The law often follows trends in society. In Holland changing the law to meet these trends has always meant tension and conflict. In the 1970's, abortion became one of the most fiercely disputed legal questions in the Netherlands. In 1984 a law was enacted stating that a woman was free to choose an abortion subject to various conditions. An abortion may be performed only by hospitals and clinics authorized to perform such an operation. Doctors must give the patient five days' time following the initial visit to reconsider her decision. Public controversy on the subject disappeared with the law's passage.

Today media coverage and public interest have shifted to the issue of mercy killing, or euthanasia. A majority of the population thinks that such a request is purely a personal choice, and euthanasia honoring that choice should be legal. Although forbidden by law in the Netherlands, in daily practice it is tolerated. Studies indicate that approximately 2,000 deaths a year in Holland are a result of euthanasia. Until a new law dealing with such deaths is passed, authorities in some cities have issued a set of practical guidelines. In Amsterdam, for example, euthanasia is permitted when the patient's suffering is unbearable, when there is no hope for recovery, and when the patient has rejected all further medical treatment and explicitly requested that his or her life be terminated.

Doctors are requested to provide detailed reports confirming when and how euthanasia was effected. Very few doctors actually comply with this request, fearing drawn-out contacts with the district attorney and possible criminal investigation. Only two hundred or so of the euthanasia cases each year are officially reported. Doctors typically designate the remaining cases "death of natural causes" on official forms. Although attorneys are aware of this pattern, active criminal investigation seldom takes place.

Some people consider the reserved attitude of Dutch prosecutors and judges too permissive, but a better description might be "pragmatic." Dutch judges realize the law must adapt to changes in medicine and society. Judges and prosecutors are not alone. Eighty-five percent of the Dutch population agrees that under certain circumstances euthanasia must be made possible.

Holland's policy toward drugs is another example of the law's response to changing society. The sale and use of hard drugs is illegal. In some Dutch cities, however, soft drugs are considered less harmful

Most Dutch cities have shops where the soft drugs hashish and marijuana are sold legally.
Photo by Theo van Stegeren

and are therefore treated separately. Possession of large quantities of soft drugs is illegal, but the sale and use of small quantities is tolerated. Amsterdam alone has some two hundred "coffee shops," where price lists on the wall indicate a wide selection of hashish and marijuana. Officials in these cities claim that their policy works. Removing soft drugs from the black market keeps prices low. Soft-drug users can pay these prices without stealing or robbing. Moreover, soft drugs are effectively separated from the world of hard drugs.

Another keynote of the Dutch drug policy is that hard-drug users are treated primarily as patients, not as criminals. Four out of five hard-drug users maintain regular contact with social workers and nurses. They receive methadone, a legal substitute for heroin, which minimizes the side effects of heroin withdrawal. Free sterile needles are also provided to help prevent the spread of AIDS and hepatitis.

What some critics prophesied has not come true. The Dutch policy toward drugs has not created an epidemic of drug abuse. Only .1 percent of the population uses hard drugs, and that number is decreasing instead of increasing. The presence of AIDS among drug users has remained remarkably low. More than in previous decades, Holland now receives international recognition for its approach to the drug problem.

· 185 ·

Leisure, Sports, and Arts

Like every modern Western society, Holland has experienced a leisure boom over the last thirty years. Dutch people now spend, on average, nearly fifty hours a week on activities other than work, education, sleep, or care for their families and households. They occupy those hours in many of the same ways as citizens of other Western countries. On a warm day the Dutch rush to the beaches along the North Sea coast, visit national parks and amusement parks, or attend sporting events and pop concerts. On cool or rainy days people often visit family and friends, go to museums, or spend their time at home, selecting from the steady flow of available television and radio programs, magazines, books, compact discs, and videocassettes.

Watching television is the most popular way to pass leisure time at all levels of Dutch society. Reading has continually increased in popularity among the better educated. An extraordinarily large number of people take vacations. In spite of the ecological consequences, the automobile is still the center of all outdoor leisure activities.

In a crowded country like Holland, it is not surprising that many people like to spend their leisure time in solitude. That solitude, unfortunately, is not easy to find. Only the very rich can afford houses with gardens. Others are fortunate enough to have small balconies or gardens, but are still forced to hear their neighbors.

To provide people with additional gardening space, cities have laid out thousands of small property allotments called *volkstuinen* (garden houses). A typical allotment provides enough space for a small garden and a tiny house to store garden tools and furniture. People rent these spaces for growing their flowers and vegetables. In spite of their modest

People working in an allotment garden.   Photo by Theo van Stegeren

Skiing has become a very popular sport among the Dutch over the last twenty years. Millions of Dutch people travel to winter resorts in more mountainous neighboring countries such as Germany, Switzerland, and Austria. Artificial slopes in Holland are used to warm up for the skiing season beforehand. Photo by Theo van Stegeren

Skutsje *sailing in Friesland.* Photo by ANP

size and often unfavorable locations, these *volkstuinen* are very popular.

With a somewhat greater effort, it is possible to find peace and quiet in the open air. But silence is often broken by the background roar of highway traffic.

No Europeans go on vacation more than the Dutch. Among citizens in the highest income group, 86 percent take vacations, and, even in the lowest income group, 50 percent do. A majority of these vacationers go abroad. France, Germany, Spain, and the Greek islands are favorite destinations. Dutch students and young people travel, with the help of numerous travel agencies, all over the world on relatively small budgets.

Sports

Sports are the second most popular way for the Dutch people to pass their leisure time. Two thirds of the Dutch population six years old and over are regularly active in sporting activities. Over the last two decades sports in Holland have changed. Sports previously participated in by the well-to-do only, like tennis, skiing, golf, and sailing, have quickly gained popularity among the general population. Relatively new sports like windsurfing and marathon walking have attracted a substantial number of enthusiasts. Most people, however, prefer individual sports practiced far away from sports facilities and associations. Swimming, fishing, hiking, biking, ice-skating, and sailing belong to this category. Soccer and tennis are the most popular organized sports.

The world of professional sports is relatively small and under-developed in Holland. Olympic medals and international champion-ships are won regularly by Dutch athletes in sports like soccer, hockey, ice-skating, swimming, bicycle racing, and rowing. A professional sports

Overleaf: *The Dutch national soccer team parades through the canals of Amsterdam after winning the European championship in 1988.*   Photo by Klaas-Jan van der Weij

career is not, however, highly valued by most Dutch people. Schools do not discourage their students from engaging in sports activities, but training schedules are not as ambitious or aggressive as those in Germany and the United States. Teachers and parents continually emphasize that education comes first above all else. Boys and girls are supposed to prepare themselves for the real world, not for a sports career. Questions like "Will it really be possible to earn a living as an athlete?" and "What will they do when their sports career is over?" come to parents' minds upon hearing that their child shows athletic promise. Even at the highest level top athletes continue, much to their later benefit, to pursue their education.

Soccer

Soccer is the sport that receives the most attention in Holland, with television providing full coverage of European and world soccer championships. Dutch pride does not come out too often, but the 1988 European soccer championship in Munich was one of those rare occasions when all reserve was laid aside. The national soccer team, with top players like Ruud Gullit, Frank Rijkaard, and Marco van Basten, had made it into the semi-finals, where it was to play against West Germany. Since World War II, soccer matches against West Germany have come to be seen as "days of reckoning," a way to settle differences with Holland's mighty neighbor.

With Holland's win over Germany (2–1), a wave of nationalism spread throughout the country. People suddenly donned orange scarves and badges (for the House of Orange) and even began to speculate on the odds of a Dutch success in the finals against the Soviet Union. That match was played on June 25 and triggered an all-time Dutch television viewer record: More than 8.5 million people, or 67 percent of the country's population, tuned in to watch the finals. The match ended in a Dutch victory (2–0). The nation's craze reached its climax in the days that followed. The players returned to a glorious welcome at home, spectators lining the entire way as the team crossed the country from the southern border all the way to Amsterdam. In the city, hundreds of thousands of people stood on quays, bridges, and houseboats to witness the team's celebrated boat tour through the canals.

Skating

Only one sports event generally receives higher television ratings than soccer. Nine out of every ten Netherlanders watched at least part of the most recent *Elfstedentocht* (Eleven City Trek) on television in 1986. The *Elfstedentocht* is a marathon ice-skating event held in the northern province of Friesland. The race can only be held when all the main canals of Friesland are frozen over. Harsh winters in Holland are unpredictable. Between 1963 and 1985 not a single *Elfstedentocht* was held. Notwithstanding, long periods of frost each winter always elicit the same national question: "Will there be an *Elfstedentocht*?" The rarity of the occasion and its dependence upon weather conditions contribute much to its almost mythical character.

Participants in the *Elfstedentocht*, men and women, start early in the morning, when it is still dark. The race then follows an extensive 125-mile-long (200-kilometer-long) course that moves through eleven Frisian towns. Hundreds of thousands of spectators cheer and supply food and drink for the skaters. Dramatic events take place throughout the race. Skaters fall, collapsing from exhaustion or from the cold. In front, small groups split off from the big pack. In each group the skaters

Overleaf: *Ice skating on a canal in Rotterdam. Photo by Rien Zilvold*   Photo by ANP

need each other's help to cut the wind and alternately take the lead. The strongest among them, however, is waiting for the opportunity to break away. The race requires a unique balance between cooperation and competition. In the *tocht* of 1956 cooperation beat out competition: The first five skaters crossed the finish line with their arms locked together.

Since the *Elfstedentocht* is usually held under harsh weather conditions, many skaters do not make it to the finish line or arrive late in the evening, their hair frozen, their fingers and toes numb. Sports commentators tend to attach deep meanings to the tour. Some interpret the course as the symbol of humanity defeating the elements; others see a direct link between the cooperative attitude of the skaters and the willingness to cooperate in Dutch society as a whole.

Television and Other Media

An average Dutch person spends twelve hours a week on television. The way houses are built in Holland is quite favorable for media broadcasting. Since most households are located either in close proximity to each other or in the same apartment building, television cable systems were easily installed throughout the country. The Netherlands possesses the most developed cable system in Europe. Of 5.9 million households, 75 percent—or 4.25 million households—are cable subscribers. By 1995 this percentage will probably have risen to 95 percent, with an expected thirty television channels available.

Newspapers and magazines are delivered to practically every Dutch home. With forty-six independent newspapers and more than 8,400 magazines, the Dutch have a wide variety to choose from. The Dutch press is a serious enterprise. While all other European countries possess daily tabloids, Holland has none. Two weeklies do tend toward the sensational. Their approach, however, is not nearly as aggressive as elsewhere in Europe. The largest daily newspaper, *De Telegraaf*, is known for its large, sensational headlines and its extensive coverage of entertainment and human-interest stories. But even this paper keeps a balance by reporting as extensively on political and social affairs and by refraining from soft pornography.

Dutch newspaper and television journalists obey an unwritten law that states that people's privacy may only be violated if the public interest demands it. The private life of politicians, for instance, is seldom reported, even when alcohol or scandals are involved. The full names or addresses of suspects and criminals are not made public. Regardless of the crime committed, hard criminals are not portrayed in newspapers or on television. Protecting the family of the accused is one reason for maintaining this standard.

The Decline of a Unique Broadcasting Structure

Broadcasting in Holland is still partly organized under the old tradition of *verzuiling*. In the early days of Dutch radio—the 1920's—every ideological and religious group was allowed to found its own broadcasting organization. These private organizations were essentially granted a monopoly on broadcasting. When television was introduced in the 1950's, the same organizations ran this new medium.

For almost fifty years the system operated successfully. Catholics were members of the Catholic Radio Broadcasting Organization (KRO), Protestants of the Dutch Christian Radio Association (NCRV) or of the Evangelical Broadcasting Organization (EO), and Socialists of the Association of Workers Radio Amateurs (VARA). More liberal-minded people united in the General Association Radio Broadcasting Organization (AVRO) or in the Liberal Protestant Radio Broadcasting Organization (VPRO). As Dutch society grew more diverse, new broadcasting organizations were set up. Moslems, humanists, various ethnic groups, and others were granted their own share of radio and TV broadcasting time. Each organization meeting the required minimum number of members (100,000) receives a broadcasting license from the government. The more members in an organization, the more broadcasting time it is granted.

By the 1970's the system began to outlive its usefulness. A younger generation of Dutch people became interested in new, nonideological broadcasting. Organizations broadcasting light entertainment soon attracted many new members and viewers. Older organizations, afraid of losing viewers, began to compromise, making their programs less recognizable as Catholic, Protestant, or Socialist.

At present the system is in a state of transition. For thirty years attempts to initiate commercial broadcasting were blocked by parliament. Since 1989, however, the Media Law permits commercial television under various conditions. At the same time, Christian political parties still veto proposals to allow advertising on Sundays on public broadcast channels. Fierce competition between newly established commercial stations and the public broadcasting system lies ahead.

Television has contributed its share to the decline of *verzuiling* in the Netherlands. From 1951 to 1964 the Netherlands operated with only one TV channel. This channel functioned as a sort of televised town meeting where all kinds of people could meet. Christians, Social Democrats, and Liberals could now get to "know" each other on television. Painful confrontations were sometimes a result. The Socialist VARA and their progressive-liberal colleagues at the VPRO were real tormentors for Christian and conservative viewers. The VPRO specialized primarily in programs in which taboos on religion, sexuality, and monarchical authority were deliberately challenged. In a satirical drama series the Queen was portrayed as an old, permed housewife peeling Brussels sprouts in the living room; the newborn child Jesus was played as an obese fellow clothed only in diapers.

One of the most traumatic events for Christian viewers in Dutch television history was an episode of the program *Zo is het toevallig ook nog eens 'n keer* (*It Also Happens to Be True*), broadcast by the VARA in 1963. This program compared Dutch society's "worship" of the television to a new "religion." Television antennae were likened to holy crosses, TV sets to altars. One commentator recited a satirical version of the Ten Commandments, quoting phrases like "Thou shalt not turn the dial, for this is an abomination of the Image," and ended with the prayer "Give us this day our daily Image."

The day following the broadcast, the Prime Minister issued a statement that the Minister of Cultural Affairs was looking at ways to prevent further episodes of the program from being broadcast. Leaders of three Christian political parties demanded that the government take harsher measures. The program's producers received a flood of scolding and threatening letters from angry viewers. In the end a written warning to the VARA from the minister himself was the only official reaction. In turn, the public's threats and complaints actually had a reverse effect, reinforcing the opinion of left-wing television producers that Holland needed to be freed from its old-fashioned ways. Consequently, a tradition of programs that modestly attacked society's taboos began in the 1960's and 1970's.

The days of one national channel are long gone. Today, cable supplies about fifteen channels to every home. Like the Dutch kitchen, Dutch television has become truly international: Programs from Belgium, Germany, France, Great Britain, Luxemburg, and Italy find their way to the

Dutch public. Cable operators also transmit MTV, Cable News Network, and the Discovery Channel from the United States. Although many viewers enjoy flipping from one channel to another, foreign channels are not yet fundamental to Dutch people's viewing habits. The four Dutch networks remain by far the most popular. These channels—three public, one commercial—together account for 85 percent of the viewers' time. More than half of their broadcasting time is filled with soap operas, sitcoms, and variety shows produced in countries like the United States, Great Britain, Germany, and Australia. *Dallas*, *Dynasty*, *Miami Vice*, *The Cosby Show*, *L.A. Law*, *Knight Rider*, *The Golden Girls*, *Cagney and Lacey*, *Rescue 911*, *The Oprah Winfrey Show*, *Geraldo*, and *America's Funniest Home Videos*: Dutch viewers have seen them all, naturally with subtitles in Dutch. Yet, in spite of these programs' popularity, the highest ratings go to Dutch drama series, game shows, news shows, and sports programs.

Arts

The arts are very much alive in Holland. Museums like the Rijksmuseum, Stedelijk Museum, Van Gogh Museum, Booijmans van Beuningen, and Kröller Müller demonstrate that the most important movements in painting have always had their Dutch representatives. The intense and personal approach to painting of Vincent van Gogh (1853–1890) gave a decisive push to Expressionism. Piet Mondriaan (1872–1944), working in an opposite, more abstract direction, influenced Constructivism. Together with the painter Theo Doesburg (1883–1931) and the architect Gerrit Rietveld (1888–1964), Mondriaan contributed to the Dutch magazine *De Stijl.* This magazine, founded in 1917, became world famous by presenting new rules and principles for artistic design. Rietveld is considered one of the most important architects of this century. His red-and-blue chair and his Rietveld-Schröder House are famous examples of the ideas formulated in *De Stijl*.

After World War II, COBRA, a group of painters from Denmark, Belgium, and the Netherlands who met regularly in the years 1948 to 1951, gave a new impetus to Expressionism. The Dutch painters Karel Appel, Corneille, and Constant were prominent in this movement.

The Nederlands Dans Theater (Dutch Dance Theater), founded in 1959, is known all over the world for its unique repertory, a mixture of classical and modern dance. Another ballet company, the Nationale Ballet (National Ballet), founded in 1961, operates on the same high level, but has concentrated on the national rather than the international stages. Three brilliant Dutch choreographers have also gained world-

The National Ballet performing on the Dam square in Amsterdam.   Photo by ANP

wide recognition: Rudi van Dantzig, Hans van Manen, and Toer van Schayk. Ballet companies throughout the world perform their works, and they have been asked to choreograph for stars like Rudolph Nureyev.

Holland has twenty-one professional orchestras, of which the Concertgebouworkest (Concert gebouw [Concert Hall] Orchestra) has become especially well known abroad. In pop and jazz music all styles are represented by thousands of groups and ensembles. Pop music played by Dutch artists, also called *Nederpop*, made its initial appearance around 1960 with the first Dutch cover versions of Everly Brothers songs. Dutch pop music has now reached a professional level. Most lyrics are sung in English, which makes them sound more impressive and a bit more mysterious. Songs in Dutch, though, have also become accepted.

The art world was turned upside down in the late 1960's, with every kind of expression experiencing its share of the "cultural revolution." Young playwrights, pop musicians, filmmakers, experimental designers, and many others made the Dutch art scene more lively and exciting than it had been for a long time. In 1969 Dutch theater came under attack. Young actors organized an "Action Tomato." During performances they started throwing tomatoes and other objects at older actors who, in their opinion, represented a conservative approach to the theater. The rise of a flourishing youth counterculture, reacting against the dominant conservative culture, was strongly felt in the arts. Between 1967 and 1973 Amsterdam was the "magical" center of that counterculture. In clubs like Mickerey (experimental theater), Paradiso, Fantasio, and De Melkweg (The Milky Way) (pop music, dance, poetry), and in numerous alternative magazines, many young artists from around the world took their first steps toward success.

The effects of the movement of the 1960's and 1970's are still visible.

Dutch Artists Abroad

For various reasons, many Dutch artists over the years have lived temporarily or permanently outside Holland. Erasmus, Multatuli, and Vincent van Gogh spent most of their time abroad. The visual artists Piet Mondriaan, Willem de Kooning, Karel Appel, and Jan Dibbets, the writer Jan de Hartog, and the poet Leo Vroman lived for various amounts of time in the United States. Two of Holland's most prominent authors, Gerard Reve and Willem F. Hermans, chose to live permanently in France.

Some of these emigrants were in search of a more adventurous life-style or had personal reasons for leaving. Living abroad they each developed a sharp eye for the shortcomings of their home country. Physicist and poet Leo Vroman, who has lived in the United States since 1946, wrote a poem called "Indian Summer" (in *126 Poems*), in which he describes his mixed feelings about the country he left behind:

> *To talk is to puff in someone's face;*
> *to gesture is to give someone a cuff.*
> *People start at the sound of a laugh,*
> *confusing proximity with hate.*
>
> *No, even groping for heath and strand*
> *(and though I may close my ear*
> *to hear Holland's storms) still I fear*
> *I'd rather have homesickness than Holland.*

In the nineteenth century, the writer Multatuli criticized his fellow countrymen for their self-satisfaction. The essayist Rudy Kousbroek, who lived in Paris one century later, worried about the Dutch lack of historical consciousness. He says their history is more interesting than they realize themselves: "Netherlanders seem imprisoned in a paper-thin 'present,' like memory-stripped rats in a maze."

Each of the arts combines its own traditional approaches with alternative solutions. Experimental film and theater as well as critical cabaret are now accepted artistic forums.

Modern Dutch literature has profited from the 1960's as well. Given the small size of the reading public, the number of published titles is enormous. Willem Frederik Hermans is widely regarded as the greatest Dutch novelist of the postwar years. Other successful authors are Simon Vestdijk, Harry Mulisch, Cees Nooteboom, Hella Haase, Gerard Reve, Jan Wolkers, and Maarten 't Hart. The international reach of Dutch books is limited because so few people read Dutch. In recent years, however, a growing number of titles have been translated into English, French, German, and other languages.

Like literature, film in the Netherlands has to accommodate itself to a limited market. Because of the relatively small audience, few feature films are profitable. In spite of that, a stream of new films is released each year with financial help from the government and other sponsors. Some of them, like Paul Verhoeven's *Soldier of Orange* (1979) and Fons Rademakers's *The Assault* (1986), were successfully introduced to international audiences. The greatest achievements of the Dutch film industry are in the documentary genre. The works of Joris Ivens and Bert Haanstra offer a many-faceted reflection of Dutch culture and society during the past fifty years. Haanstra (*Mirror of Holland*, 1950; *Rembrandt, Painter of Men*, 1956; *Fanfare*, 1959; *The Human Dutch*, 1963; *The Voice of the Water*, 1966) focuses on the Dutch people and their foibles. Ivens (*The Bridge*, 1928; *Indonesia Calling*, 1946; *Rotterdam Europoort*, 1965; *How Yukong Moved the Mountains*, 1976) takes a more critical approach toward his subjects.

All the arts—from film and literature to pop and jazz—are in part subsidized by the government. That dependence makes the position of the artist vulnerable. And some art forms, like theater, suffer from the fact that going out to performances does not come as easy to the Dutch as, say, to the French. The natural habitat of the people remains in and about the home, where life still shows signs of the bourgeois culture that emerged in previous centuries. A thriving Dutch cultural life can be found in Amsterdam and Rotterdam, but in the rest of the country theaters often have a hard time surviving.

Holland's Future

Although few nations seem to offer their citizens sunnier prospects than Holland, a cloud has appeared over its future. The amazing economy is taking its toll. Rivers, soil, air, sea, and forests are all seriously affected by pollution.

The Netherlands is located in the delta region of a highly industrialized Western Europe. The country is also very densely populated. Pollution problems consequently make themselves felt sooner and more seriously than in other countries. Existing incinerators have reached their maximum capacity. Several plants designated as presenting direct danger to people's health have been closed by authorities. Big cities are in turn desperately seeking new ways to dispose of household garbage.

Poisoned Environment

The chemical industry has been hit with the same issue. Dangerous waste products, containing cancer-causing agents like dioxin and cadmium, have been dumped illegally throughout the country. Authorities have either pretended not to know or refrained from taking effective control. Over the last decade, more than eight thousand waste sites have been designated as immediate health hazards and fenced off from the public. Entire neighborhoods of towns built on polluted soil have been and will have to be demolished, costing hundreds of millions of dollars per year.

Wildlife in De Hoge Veluwe National Park   Photo from Cas Oorthuys archive

Dutch rivers and canals have also been poisoned by pollution. Industries in France, Germany, Switzerland, Belgium, and Holland dump chemical wastes such as benzene and cadmium into the Rhine, Meuse, and Scheldt rivers. Agriculture contributes additional tons of pesticides and herbicides. Cleaning the riverbeds will mean an expenditure of several billion dollars.

Tens of millions of pigs, cows, and chickens have transformed large parts of the country into dunghills. The province of North Brabant—the heart of Dutch cattle breeding—has built up more than six million tons of dung residue. Ammonia released from the dung adds significantly to the acidity of the air and soil. Any passerby will easily recognize the smell of ammonia rising from fields and ditches. Forests in the Netherlands lack the vitality of their past. Of all trees in Holland, only half (50.9 percent) are still judged healthy. The rest are designated as unhealthy (28.1 percent), ill (16 percent), or dead (5 percent).

Pollution has officially been declared the Netherlands' number-one problem. The government has developed a National Plan for Environmental Protection proposing drastic measures. Industry, agriculture, car owners—virtually everyone—will be confronted with higher taxes and painful new restrictions.

As yet, the population has not been completely assured of a sound environmental future. According to the government, even with the implementation of the National Plan, large portions of North Brabant and Limburg will still be "seriously threatened" in the year 2010, while the main part of the country will remain "moderately threatened." Facing the 1990's, 65 percent of Dutch high school students said their largest concern was ecology. This awareness is gradually being converted into action, which indeed is hopeful. Membership in ecological organizations like Greenpeace and the World Wildlife Fund is quickly rising.

With environmental pollution accelerating the elimination of wildlife species, the Dutch government has come to understand the seriousness of the situation. Steps have been taken to protect surviving species and to reintroduce species no longer present in the Netherlands. Reintroducing the beaver is one example of such a campaign. This animal was hunted for its precious fur for centuries, until 1825, when the last beaver in Holland was killed. One hundred sixty years later, the Ministry of Agriculture and Fisheries imported six new beavers from East Germany and relocated them at the Biesbosch National Park. Small transmitters implanted in their abdominal cavities send radio signals to rangers, who in turn study their behavior. The aim of the project is to promote the species' population growth and thereby return the beaver to Holland as a permanent inhabitant.

Holland's need for energy poses many environmental problems. Development of nuclear power plants was halted after massive protest demonstrations during the 1970's. Enormous windmill projects are planned to provide the country with clean energy. Private citizens too are taking their own small-scale initiatives to help make a cleaner world. When seen in broader perspective, the country appears to be in the middle of a giant U-turn from unchecked development to an ecologically sound future. The next two decades will show whether it can make the transition.

The European Community

With an eye on Holland's future, a second topic causes some anxiety among the Dutch: the position of Holland within Europe. The country is a member of the European Community, a collective name for three multinational organizations that cooperate in various ways, the European Economic Community being one of them. The EC now has twelve member states. Starting in 1993, national borders between the member nations will be gradually abolished. People, commodities, services, and money will be allowed to move freely from one country to another. Crucial political and economic decisions will no longer be made in the national capitals, but in the capitals of the European Community: Brussels, Strasbourg, or Luxemburg. For smaller countries like Portugal, Denmark, Belgium, and the Netherlands, this will be the moment of truth. Language, art, religion, and ideals will become the only areas in which these countries can express their own identities. Even these domains, however, are endangered. The Dutch language, for instance, will have little standing among the languages that dominate international contacts: English, French, German, and Spanish. The arts in Holland will be more dependent upon European funding, in which larger European countries will have greater influence. The country's broadcasting system will face full competition with foreign television and radio stations. The tolerant policies applied to criminal law and drugs will be placed under greater pressure from other, more restrictive countries like Germany and Great Britain. In short, Holland will be forced to defend its historic achievements more than ever before.

Pessimists fear that Holland will become the "Friesland" of Europe. The Netherlands, they suggest, will simply become one of many European provinces where people have nothing to cling to other than an isolated language and folklore. An alleged lack of enthusiasm among the Dutch for their own history, language, and culture leads some to believe that Holland's international orientation will ultimately lead to a complete immersion in German, British, French—and American—influences.

Other people feel less threatened. Holland's international orientation, they argue, could prove to be its strength. The Dutch have always been open to foreign cultures, have communicated in other languages, and are accustomed to working within multinational corporations. Precisely their lack of nationalism, willingness to cooperate, and ultimate pragmatism will enable the Netherlands to adapt to the new situation in Europe more quickly than other countries can, while at the same time preserving its own national identity.

Bibliography

Books that are easier to read are marked with an asterisk (*).

General

*Hopkins, Adam. *Holland: Its History, Paintings and People.* Boston: Faber, 1988.

Huggett, Frank E. *The Modern Netherlands.* New York: Praeger, 1971.

**The Kingdom of the Netherlands: Facts and Figures.* The Hague: Ministry of Foreign Affairs, 1989.

**The Netherlands in Brief.* The Hague: Ministry of Foreign Affairs, 1987.

Newton, Gerald. *The Netherlands: An Historical and Cultural Survey, 1795–1977.* Boulder, CO: Westview Press, 1978.

Shetter, William Z. *The Netherlands in Perspective: The Organizations of Society and Environment.* Leiden: Martinus Nijhoff, 1987.

Tamsma, R. *The Netherlands in Fifty Maps: An Annotated Atlas.* Amsterdam: Royal Dutch Geographical Society, 1988.

The Dutch and Their Land

Barzini, Luigi. *The Europeans,* Chapter 3: "The Careful Dutch." New York: Simon & Schuster, 1983.

De Amicis, Edmondo. *Holland and Its People.* New York: Putnam, 1882.

Goudsblom, Johan. *Dutch Society.* New York: Random House, 1967.

Lambert, Audrey M. *The Making of the Dutch Landscape: An Historical Geography of the Netherlands.* New York: Seminar, 1971.

Temple, William. *Observation upon the United Provinces of the Netherlands.* Ed. George Clark. Oxford: Clarendon, 1972.

*White, Colin, and Laurie Boucke. *The Undutchables, an Observation of the Netherlands: Its Culture and Its Inhabitants.* Montrose, CA: Colin White & Laurie Boucke, 1989.

Language and Early History

Boxer, C. R. *The Dutch Seaborne Empire: 1600–1800.* New York: Knopf, 1965.

Brachin, P. *The Dutch Language: A Survey.* London: Thornes, 1985; Leiden: Brill, 1985.

Braudel, Fernand. *Civilization and Capitalism in the Fifteenth to the Eighteenth Century*, Vol. 3: *The Perspective of the World*, Chapter 3: "The City-Centered Economies of the European Past." New York: Harper & Row, 1984.

Faludy, George. *Erasmus of Rotterdam.* London: Eyre & Spottiswode, 1970.

Geyl, Pieter. *The Netherlands in the 17th Century, 1609–1648.* New York: Barnes & Noble, 1961.

Huizinga, Johan. *Dutch Civilization in the Seventeenth Century and Other Essays.* London: Harper & Row, 1968.

*Parker, Geoffrey. *The Dutch Revolt.* New York: Viking Penguin, 1985.

*Schama, Simon. *The Embarrassment of Riches: An Interpretation of Dutch Culture in the Golden Age.* New York: Knopf, 1986.

Modern History

Kossman, E. H. *The Low Countries.* Oxford: Oxford University Press, 1978.

Lijphart, Arend. *The Trauma of Decolonization: The Dutch and West Guinea.* New Haven: Yale University Press, 1966.

Maass, Walter B. *The Netherlands at War 1940–1945*. New York and London: Abelard-Schumann, 1970.

Palmier, Leslie H. *Indonesia and the Dutch*. London and New York: Oxford University Press, 1962.

*Presser, Jacob. *The Destruction of the Dutch Jews*. New York: Dutton, 1969.

Rowen, Herbert H., ed. *The Low Countries in Early Modern Times: A Documentary History*. New York: Harper & Row, 1972.

*Schama, Simon. *Patriots and Liberators: Revolution in the Netherlands 1780–1813*. New York: Knopf, 1977.

Contemporary Affairs

Barnes, S. H., and M. Kaase, eds. *Political Action: Mass Participation in Five Western Democracies*. Beverly Hills and London: Sage, 1979.

Daalder, H., and P. Mair. *Western European Party Systems: Continuity and Change*. London: Sage, 1983.

Fry, Earl H., and Gregory A. Raymond. *The Other Western Europe: A Political Analysis of the Smaller Democracies*, 2nd ed. Santa Barbara, CA: ABC-Clio Information Services, 1983.

Lijphart, Arend. *The Politics of Accommodation: Pluralism and Democracy in the Netherlands*, 2nd ed. Berkeley: University of California Press, 1975.

Arts and Literature

Barnouw, A. J. *Coming After: An Anthology of Poetry from the Low Countries*. New Brunswick: Rutgers University Press, 1948.

Friedman, Mildred, ed. *De Stijl, 1917–1931: Visions of Utopia*. New York: Abbeville, 1982.

Fuchs, R. H. *Dutch Painting*. London: Thames & Hudson, 1989.

Greshoff, Jan. *Harvest of the Lowlands: An Anthology in English Translation of Creative Writing in the Dutch Language with a Historical Survey of the Literary Development*. New York: Querido, 1945.

*Haak, B. *The Golden Age: Dutch Painters of the Seventeenth Century*. New York: Abrams, 1984.

Price, J. L. *Culture and Society in the Dutch Republic During the 17th Century*. London: B. T. Batsford Ltd., 1974.

Dutch Literature Translated into English
19th Century

*Couperus, Louis. *Old People and the Things That Pass.* (Bibliotheca Neerlandica.) Leiden: Sijthoff, 1963; London: Heinemann, 1963.

*Emants, Marcellus. *A Posthumous Confession.* (Library of Netherlandic Literature, Vol. 7.) New York: Twayne, 1975.

*Multatuli, pseud. *Max Havelaar.* (Library of The Indies.) Amherst: University of Massachusetts, 1982.

Van Eeden, Frederik. *The Deeps of Deliverance.* (Library of Netherlandic Literature, Vol. 5.) New York: Twayne, 1975.

A selection of Dutch literature on the Indies is published and reprinted in the series Library of the Indies, edited by E. M. Beekman and published by the University of Massachusetts Press at Amherst.

World War II in Literature

*Frank, Anne. *The Diary of a Young Girl.* New York: Pan Books, 1954.

*———. *Tales from the Secret Annex.* New York: Washington Square Press, 1983.

*Hermans, Willem Frederik. *The Dark Room of Damocles.* London: Heinemann, 1962.

*Hillesum, Etty. *An Interrupted Life: The Diaries of Etty Hillesum 1941–1943.* New York: Washington Square Press, 1983.

*Minco, Marga. *Bitter Herbs: A Little Chronicle.* New York: Pergamon, 1969.

*Mulisch, Harry. *The Assault.* New York: Pantheon, 1985.

*———. *The Stone Bridal Bed.* London and New York: Abelard-Schumann, 1962.

Other Modern Literature and Poetry

*Blaman, Anna. *A Matter of Life and Death.* (Library of Netherlandic Literature, Vol. 3.) New York: Twayne, 1974.

Bordewijk, F. *Character.* London: Peter Owen, 1966.

*Campert, Remco. *The Gangster Girl.* London: Hart-Davies, 1968.

Cremer, Jan. *Jan Cremer.* New York: Shorecrest, 1965.

Haasse, Hella. *In a Dark Wood Wandering.* Chicago: Academy Chicago Publications, Chicago Ill. 1989.

Hart, Martin. *Bearers of Bad Tidings.* New York: Schocken, 1985.

———. *Rats.* New York: Schocken, 1982.

Hermans, Willem Frederik. *Sleep No More.*

Holmes, James S., and William Jay Smith, eds. *Dutch Interior: Postwar Poetry of the Netherlands and Flanders.* New York: Columbia University Press, 1984.

Nooteboom, Cees. *Rituals.* Baton Rouge, LA: Louisiana State University Press, 1984.

———. *A Song of Truth and Semblance.* Baton Rouge, LA: Louisiana State University Press.

*———. *In the Dutch Mountains.* New York: Viking Penguin, 1987.

*Van Schendel, Arthur. *The Waterman.* (Bibliotheca Neerlandica.) Leiden: Sijthof, 1963; London: Heinemann, 1963.

Schierbeek, Bert. *Shapes of the Voice.* (Library of Netherlandic Literature.) New York: Twayne, 1977.

*Wolkers, Jan. *Turkish Delight.* New York and Boston: Seymour Lawrence and Delacorte, 1974.

Filmography

The Netherlands Ministry of Foreign Affairs (Foreign Information Service, Audio-Visual Section, P.O. Box 20061, 2500 EB The Hague, Netherlands) produces an annual catalog of documentaries on the Netherlands. This detailed English-language guide lists offerings in a variety of formats on many of the subjects covered in this book.

Index

References to illustrations are in *italics*.

Aalsmeer, 140
abortion, 13, 183–84
action groups, 13, 45, 163–64, 167
Afsluitsdijk. *See* Barrier Dam
agriculture, 49–50, 83, 140, 141, 143,
    146, 149–50, *149*, *150*, 208
    See also farming
AIDS, 179, 185
American Revolutionary War, 117
Amsterdam, *2*, 14, *18*, 22, 26, 28, 30,
    34, 40, 63, 64, 90, *92*, 97, 98,
    107, 108, 110, 114, 116, 118,
    128, 130, 139, 176, 193, *201*,
    202, 205
Angles, settlement by, 76, 77
Antilles, 63, 122, 137
Anti-Revolutionary Party, 120, 122,
    149
Antwerp, 81, 89, 93, 114
Appel, Karel, 201, 203
Arnhem, 132
arts, 81, 97, *99*, 107–13, *109*, *110*,
    112, 200–5, 210
Association for Female Suffrage,
    124
atheism, 104
automobiles, 4, 9–10, 53, 163, 187,
    208

Baltic Sea, 80, 84
banking, 92
Barrier Dam, 25, 42–43
Basten, Marco van, 192
"Batavian Republic," 117
Beatrijs, medieval poem about, 79–80
Beatrix, Queen, 13, 156, 157, *157*,
    165
Belgium, 3, 74, 76, 81, 89, 118–19,
    125, 126, 199, 201, 208, 210
bicycles, 17, 49, 53–54, *54*, 125, 127,
    189
Biesbosch National Park, 23, 30, 209
black market, 175–76, *176*
Blood Council, 85–87
Bomans, Godfried, 11
Bontekoe, Johan, diary of, 105–6
Bosch, Hieronymous, 81
Bosman, Willem, 94, 96
Bruges, 81, 89, 114
Brussels, 81, 210
Burgundian Empire, 119
    Hapsburg royal family, 84–85
    language, mix of, 81
    merchants and nobles, conflict
        between, 80–81
    nobility, decline in power of, 80
    political unity, lack of, 81

textile industry, 81
trading towns, rise of, 80
business sense, 16–17

Caesar, Julius, 72
Calvinism, 11, 33, 85, 104, 118, 120
canals, *2*, 5, 23, 25, 31, 34, 41, 52, 92, *92*, 189, *193*, 208
capitalism, 104
capital punishment, 180
Carolingian Empire (Holy Roman Empire), 77, 84
Catholicism. *See* Roman Catholicism
Catholic People's Party, 121, 122, 159
    See also Christian Democratic Alliance
character of the Dutch people
    business sense, 16–17
    conformity, desire for, 10–11
    contradictions, 15
    daily routines, 49–61, *51*, 64, 98, 99, 112
    driving habits, 3, 53–54
    eating habits, 51, *51*, 60–61
    ecology, concern for, 45–46, 206–9
    emotions, 7, 11
    ethics, 12–14, 56
    gezellig thuis, 7–8, 64
    gift giving, 11
    home and family, importance of, 7–8, 64
    industriousness, 5, 19–20, 138, 139, 141, 151–52
    liberalization of attitudes, 15
    merchant as representative type, 19–20, 97, 140
    money, attitude toward, 11–12, 151–52, 171

physical appearance, 9
preacher as representative type, 19–20, 97, 140
privacy, value of, 5–7, 175, 182, 197
reserved attitude, 5–7, 11, 182
style, sense of, 9–10
tolerance of differences, 9, 14–15, 16, 17–18, 34, 50, 122, 124–25, 142, 210
volunteerism, 13
wealth, attitude toward, 11–12
work ethic, 5, 19–20, 104, 138, 139, 140, 141, 145, 151–52
world affairs, interest in, 1–2
Charlemagne, 73, 77–79
child care, 57–59
child labor laws, 122–24
children, 49, 50, 51, 54–55, 57, 58–59, 62, 64, 65, 98, 122, 124, 151–52, 178, 180
Christian Democratic Alliance, 155, 158
Christianity, conversion of Netherlands to, 77
churches, *78*, 82–83, *83*
city life, 29, 50
class, 9, 12, 54–55, 90, 100, 116, 171, 175, 177
Claus, Prince, 13, *157*, 165
clothing styles, 9
Colet, John, 102
colonies, 122, 123
    loss of, 135–37
colonization of America, 91
commuting, daily, 52–54
concentration camps, 127–30, *129*
conformity, desire for, 10–11
Constant, 201
constitutions, 118, 119–20

conurbation, 28
Coornhert, Dirck Volckertsz, 106,
    179–80
Corneille, 201
crime, handling of, 14, 16–17, 178,
    179–83, *181*, 184–85, *185*, 210
Cuba, 94

daily life, 49–61, *51*, 64, 98, 99, 112
dams, 40, 45, 46
damsteden, 40
dance, 201–2, *201*
decline of Dutch empire, 115–16,
    135–37, 138
de Groot, Huig, 97, 106–7, 143
de Hartog, Jan, 203
De Hoge Veluwe National Park, 25,
    207
Dekker, Eduard Douwes, 123, 203
de Kooning, Willem, 203
Delft, 28, 88
Deltaplan, flood prevention and, 44–47
democracy, 153, *154*, 156–61
Democrats 1966, 155, 158
de Ruyter, Michiel, 98
Deventer, 22, 80
Dibbets, Jan, 203
dikes, 23, 31, 37, 39, 40, 43, 45, 88
dissent, religious and political, 85–87,
    89, 103–4, 120, 161–67
Doesburg, Theo, 200
Drees, Willem, 168
Drenthe province, 29
drinking habits, 110, 111
driving habits, 3, 53–54
    See also automobiles
drugs, illegal, 14, 17, 179, 184–85,
    185, 210
dunes, 23, *24*, 30, 48

Dutch East India Company. *See* VOC
Dutch East Indies. *See* Indonesia
Dutch empire, 1, 90–94, 104, 114,
    123
    decline of, 115–16, 135–37, 138
Dutch Union, 127

East Indies. *See* Indonesia
eating habits, 51, *51*, 60–61, 98
    See also food
ecology, 45–46, 48, 206–9
economy, 1, 7, 11, 40, 80–81
    agriculture, 49–50, 83, 140, 143,
        146, 149–50, *149*, *150*. *See also*
        farming
    employment, levels of, 139
    environment, impact on, 45–46,
        206–9
    European Community, future in,
        209–10
    fishing industry, 4–5, 30, 83–84,
        144
    flower industry, 45, 95, 140
    foreign investment, 12, 151
    foreign trade, 5, 40, 84, 90–96,
        107, 114, 118, 125, 138, 141,
        143, 151, 210
    growth of, 97, 104, 138–39, 143
    industry, heavy, 141–42, 143, 144,
        146–49
    multinational corporations, 11, 135,
        138, 146, 147–48
    petroleum, 5, 28
    pollution, 206–9
    ports, importance of, 144, 145–46,
        145
    post–World War II struggle, 141–43
    poverty, presence of, 139, 168–79
    shadow economy, 175–76, *176*

shipping industry, 40, 80, 84, 89, 90–96, 138, 144–46
trucking industry, 143, *144*
unemployment, 57
United States, trade with, 151
work ethic, 5, 19–20, 138, 139, 141, 151–52
world center of, 11, 14
Edam, 40
education, *18*, 54–57, 106, 120, 121, 124, 169, 173, 176, 183, 192
Eighty Years War, 87–89, 99, 103, 104, *112*, 114
Eindhoven, 139, 148
elections, 156–61
Elfstedentocht, 193–96
emigration, 141
employment, 57, 139, 140, 174, 176
England, *77*, 89, 115, 116, 126, 174, 199–200, 210
Enkuizen, 22, 90
entertainment, 6–8, 64–67
environmental issues. *See* ecology
Erasmus, Desiderius, 97, 101–3, *101*, 104, 106, 112, 203
European Community (EC), 20, 144, 209–10
European Economic Community (EEC), 137, 143, 209
See also European Community
Europoort Rotterdam, *145*, 146
euthanasia, 8, 13, 184

farming, 21, 25, 31, 41, 42, 43, 45, 49, 80, 146–50
See also agriculture
feudal period, 79–80, 84
Catholic Church, power of, 77–80
military violence, 77, 79

serfs, life of, 79
films, 202, 204
fishing industry, 4–5, 30, 83–84, 144
Flanders, 79–80, 81, 82, 84, 88, 89, 116, 119, 126
Flemish language, 74–75, 76
Flevopolders province, 29
flooding, 37–39, 44–45
Barrier Dam, 25, 42–43
Deltaplan, 44–47
See also water
flower industry, 45, 83, 95, 138, 140
fluyt, innovation of, 84
Flying Dutchman, 33
foreign policy, 125, 137, 209–10
foreign trade, 5, 40, 84, 90–96, 107, 114, 118, 125, 138, 141, 143, 151, 210
VOC (United East India Company), 91–94
WIC (West Indies Company), 94–96
food, 8, 51, 60–61, 65, 98
forests, 206, 208
France, 24, 81, 89, 115–16, 117–18, 174, 199, 208
Frank, Anne, 127–30, *129*
Franklin, Benjamin, 113
Franks, 73–76, *77*, 80
See also Carolingian Empire
Free University, 122
French language, 76
Friesland province, 23, 25, 29, 37, 43, *50*, 75, 81, 89, 188, 193, 210
Frisian language, 74–75
Frisians, settlement by, 72, 76, 77

garden allotments, 187–89, *187*
Gelderland, 29, 79, 80, 81, 89

General Assistance Act, 170, 172, 175
geography, 2–3, 21–35, 36–48
German tribes, settlement by, 76, *76*
Germany, 3, 25, 81, 119, 125–34,
   143, 192, 199–200, 208, 210
   See also World War II
gezellig thuis, 7–8, 64
Ghent, 81, 88, 89
Giethoorn, 34
glaciers, 24, 48
Golden Age, 1, 90, 97–113
   children, status of, 98
   daily life, 98, *99*, 112
   decline of Dutch empire, 115–16
   de Groot, Huig, 97, 106–7, 143
   economy, growth of, 97, 104
   Erasmus, Desiderius, 97, 101–3,
      101, 104, 112
   family, importance of, *99*
   freedom of speech, 107
   free trade, 107
   government, 98
   humanism, 97, 102–3, 106
   international law, foundations for,
      107
   new, 138, 209–10
   painting, *99*, 107–13, *109*, *110*,
      112
   protest, political and religious,
      103–4
   religion, *99*, 104, 105
   Rembrandt van Rijn, 97, 108,
      110–11
   Steen, Jan, 108
   trade, 92
   Vermeer, Johannes, 97, 108, *109*
   women, status of, 98
Gouda, 22
government, 17–18, 98, 118, 119–20,
   122, 153–61

great rivers region, 23–24
"Green Heart" of Holland, 28–30
"greenhouse effect," 48
Groningen province, 25, 29, 37, 69,
   89, 139
Grotius, Hugo. *See* de Groot, Huig
growth of economy, 97, 104, 138–39,
   143
guilds, 82
Gulf War, 137
Gullit, Ruud, 192

Haarlem, 28
Hague, The, 28, 126, 139, 153
Hals, Frans, 95, 108
Hanseatic League, 80–82
Hapsburg royal family, 84–85
Harderwijk, 80
health care, 124, 168–69, 170,
   176
Hermans, Willem F., 203, 204
Heyn, Piet, 94
high Netherlands, 24–25
Hillesum, Etty, 127
Hilversum, 28
Hitler, Adolf, 125
Hobbema, Meindert, 108
holidays, 7–8, 64, 65–66, *66*
Holland, country of. *See* Netherlands
holland (origin of name), 39
Holland provinces, 3, 25, 29, 43, 79,
   82, 89, 90, 118
   See also North Holland, South
      Holland
Holocaust, 127–30
Holy Roman Empire. *See* Carolingian
   Empire
home and family, importance of, 7–8,
   64

homosexuality, 14, 56, 122
Hoofddorp, *8*
Hoorn, 22, 90, 105
houseboats, *2*, 5
housing, 124, 141, 164, *165*, 168–69,
    170, 172, 174, 176–78, *177*
Hudson, Henry, 91
Hudson River, discovery of, 91
humanism, 97, 102–3, 106
hutspot, 61, 88

immigrants, 62–63
independence, Dutch, 99, 114, 116,
    119–20
Indonesia, 63, 122, 123, 125, 126,
    135, *136*, 164
industriousness, 5, 19–20, 138, 139,
    141, 151–52
industry, heavy, 141–42, 143, 144,
    146–49
Inquisition, Spanish, 85–87

Jacobs, Aletta, 124
James II, King of England, 115
Japan, 1, 4, 12, 91, 151
Jews, 104, 107, 127–30, *128*, 132,
    133
John Paul II, Pope, 165–66
Juliana, Queen, 13, 157

Kampen, 80
Kan, Wim, 8–9
Kinderdijk, 39
Koninginnedag, *66*, 67
Kousbroek, Rudy, 203
Kuyper, Abraham, 120–22, *121*, 159,
    161

Labor Party, 155, 159, 168
land reclamation, 21, 23, 25, 31,
    40–43, 100
    See also water
languages
    Burgundian Empire, 81
    currently spoken, 2, 210
    Dutch, origins of, 76
    Flemish, 76
    French, 76
    Frisian, 74–75
    Germanic, influence of, 76
    under William I, 118
Latin American colonies, 63, 93, 96,
    135–37
Leiden, 22, 28, 87–88, 108
leisure time, 28, 52, 64, 172, 182,
    186–89
Lely, Cornelis, 42–43
life-styles, 15, 16, 51, 58–59, 61, 81,
    85, 199, 205
Limburg province, 22, *26*, 29, *78*,
    119, 208
literature, 32–33, 79–80, 105–6, 123,
    129–30, 141, 179–80, 203, 204
Lothair I, King, 79
Louis XIV, King of France, 115
Low Countries. *See* Netherlands
Luther, Martin, 85, 102
Lutherans, 103
Luxemburg, 119, 199, 210

Maastricht, 22, *78*
Malines (Mechlin), 81
Manhattan Island, 91
marriage, 15, 152
Marshall Plan, 142
Marsman, Hendrik, 32
mass media, 186, 196–97, 210

Maurice, Prince, 90
Mennonites, 104
merchant as representative type,
    19–20, 97, 140
Meuse River, 34, 208
Middelburg, 22, 90
military preparedness, 125
monarchs, 144–45, 158, 199
    See also royal family
monarchy, central, adoption of, 118
Mondriaan, Piet, 200, 203
money, attitude toward, 11–12,
    151–52, 171
Monnikendam, 40
moors, 25
More, Thomas, 102
Moslems, 56, 62, 198
Multatuli. *See* Dekker
multiethnic society, 62–63, *62*, *63*
multinational corporations, 11, 135,
    138, 139, 146, 147–48, 210
museums, 200,
music, 202, 204
Mussert, Anton, 126

Napoleon Bonaparte, 117–18
National Geographic, 44
National Socialist Movement, 126
National Water Affairs Department,
    47–48
Native Americans, 91
Nazis. *See* World War II
Netherlands
    appearance 2000 years ago, *73*
    Belgium, secession of, 118–19
    earliest ancestors of today's
        inhabitants, 73
    government, 17–18, 98, 118,
        119–20, 122, 153–61

name of country, 1
prehistory of, 68–72
social welfare system, 151, 168–73
women, status of, 16, 56–60, 79,
    98, 103, 124
neutrality, 125, 137
New Amsterdam, 93
newspapers, 122, 131–32, 196–97
New Year's Eve, 7
nobility, decline in power of, 80
Nooteboom, Cees, 33, 204
North Atlantic Treaty Organization
    (NATO), 137, 167
North Brabant province, 29, 79, 119,
    139, 208
northern provinces, first unification of,
    89
North Holland province, *8*, 25, 29, 43
    See also Holland provinces
North Sea, 3, 25, 42, 43, 84, 146, 186

Oosterschelde Dam, 45–47, *46*, *53*
Oosterschelde inlet ecosystem,
    protection of, 45–46
Orange, House of, 116, 119, 157, 192
    See also specific names
Overijssel, 29, 80, 81, 89

Pacification of Ghent, 88
pagan practices, elimination of, 77
painting, 22, 81, 97, *99*, 107–13,
    109, *110*, *112*, 200–1, 203
parliamentary democracy, 17–19,
    119–20, 153–55, 156–60, 167
Patriotten (patriots), 117, 118
People's Party for Freedom and
    Democracy, 155, 158
petroleum, 5, 28

Philip II, King of Spain, 85, 87, 89,
103
physical appearance of Dutch people, 9
plants, wild, 30
platteland, 22, 49
pluralism, 124–25
polders, 22–23, 25, 42, 43, 100, 142
police, 14, 16–17, 164, *165*, *166*, 167
political parties, 60, 120, 154–58,
154, 163, 198, 199
pollution, 45–46, 206–9
popes, 8, 79, 85, 165–66
population density, 4, 6, 28, 50, 141
ports, importance of, 144, 145–46,
145
Portugal, 5, 7, 84, 210
Potter, Paulus, 108
poverty, 139, 168–79, *174*
preacher as representative type, 19–20,
97, 140
prehistory, 68–72, *76*
prisons, 179–83, *181*
privacy, value of, 5–7, 175, 182,
197
prostitution, 14, 124
proportional representation, 158
Protestants, persecution of, 85–87,
89
protests, 163, 164–67
public housing, 176–78, *177*
See also housing

racism, 63, *63*, 65
Randstad Holland, 28, 132, *133*
Reformation, 84–85
regenten, 90, 116
religion, 7, 8, 11, 12, 15, 16, 31,
56–57, 77–80, 82, 84–87, 88,
89, 98, 99, *99*, 101, 102, 103,
104, 105, 106, 108, 118, 140,
142, 155, 161–63, 197, 198,
199
Rembrandt van Rijn, 95, 97, 108–12,
110
Republic of the Seven United
Netherlands, 90, 108, 114,
116–17
reserved attitude, 5–7, 11, 182
Reve, Gerard Kornelis van het, 141,
203, 204
Rhenen, archeological discoveries in,
68
Rhine River, 34, *76*, 132, 208
Rietveld, Gerrit, 200–1
Rijkaard, Frank, 192
Rijkswaterstaad (National Water
Affairs), 47–48
See also water, *waterschappen*
Rijnsburg, 140, 145
Rijnvos, Kees, 142
river delta region, 23
rivers, 21, 23–24, 34, 37, 39, 43, 206,
208
See also water
roads, 4, 9, *10*, 26, 28, 34, 53, 178
Roman Catholicism, 16, 56, 84–87,
88, 89, 101, 102, 104, 106, 108,
115, 121, 161, 162, 166, 197,
198
Roman empire, 72, 84
Romanesque church, example of, *78*
Rotterdam, 11, 28, 40, 63, 97, 101,
101, 118, 126, 139, 145–46,
145, 163, 205
royal family, 12, 13, 67, 79, 87–89,
90, 103, 115–16, 118–19, 126,
155–56, 165
Ruisdael, Jacob and Salomon van, 108
rural life, 49–50

sailing, *50*, *188*, 189
St. Elizabeth's flood, 39
Saxons, settlement by, 73, 76, 77
Scheldt River, 34, 89, 208
Schendel, Arthur, 33
sea. *See* water
serfs, life of, 79
shipping industry, 40, 80, 84, 89,
  90–96, 138, 144–46
  VOC (Dutch East India Company),
    91–94
  WIC (West Indies Company),
    94–96
shipwreck, account of, 105–6
skating, 52, 189, 193–96, *194–95*
skiing, *188*, 189
skutsjes (sailboats), *50*, *188*
slave trade, 94–96
soccer, 189, *190–91*, 192–93
Socialists, 12, 124, 161–62, 168, 197,
  198
social life, 9
social reforms, 122, 124
social welfare system, 151, 168–79
soil types, 23–28, *29*
South Africa, 74
South Holland, 29, 45, *150*
  See also Holland provinces
South Limburg, *26*
Spain, 39, 84, 85–89, 90, 99, 101,
  103, 104–5, 172
Spinoza, Baruch, 107
sports, *50*, 52, 186, *188*, 189–96,
  190–91, *194–95*
States General, 87, 153–55, 156
Steen, Jan, *99*, 108
Strasbourg, 210
student loans, 173
Surinam, 63, 93, 96, 135–37
Switzerland, 24, 208

taxes, 85, 99, 118, 120, 151, 170,
  173, 175–76
technology, 5, 146–50
television, 142, 186, 192–93,
  196–200, 210
tennis, 189
terpen, 37, *69*, 72
textile industry, 81
theater, 202, 204–5
Third World, 13, 14
Thorbecke, Johan Rudolf, 119–20
tolerance and cooperation, value of, 9,
  14–15, 16, 17–18, 34, 50, 106,
  122, 124–25, 142, 210
trade. *See* foreign trade
trade unions, 60, 124, 143, 168
trading towns, rise of, 80
transportation, 21, 28, 52–54, 127,
  138
  See also cars
Treaty of Munster, 114
Treaty of Rastadt, 116
Treaty of Utrecht, 116
trucking industry, 143, *144*
tulips, 23, 95
  See also flower industry

unemployment, 57, 139, 169
Union of Utrecht, 89
urban renewal, 178
  See also housing
United States, trade with, 151
Utrecht, 28
Utrecht province, 29, 79, 89
Uylenburgh, Saskia van, 108

Vaalserberg, 22
van Gogh, Vincent, 200, 203

Veen, Herman van, 58
Veere, 22, 90
Velde, Willem van de, de Oude, 112
Veluwe, 25
Vermeer, Johannes, 97, 108, *109*
verzuiling, 122, 161–63, 197, 198
Vluwe region, 25
VOC (United East India Company),
   91–94
Volendam, 40
volunteerism, 13
Vondel, Joost van den, 98
voting rights and habits, 120, 124,
   160–61
Vroman, Leo, 203

Wadden Sea, 25, 30
War of the Grand Alliance, 116
wars, 39, 77, 87–88, 106–116
   See also specific war
waste disposal, 206, 207
water
   influence on life, 4–5, 23–24,
     30–34, 100, 144, 206
   struggle to control, 5, *24*, 25,
     30–48, 104–5
waterbikes, *2*
waterschappen (water boards), 18, 31,
   100, 153
wealth, 9, 11–12, 170, 171
Weber, Max, 104
Westland, 140, *150*
WIC (West Indies Company), 93,
   94–96
wildlife, 25, 28–30, 68, *207*, 208–9
Wilhelmina, Queen, 126, 157

William and Mary, monarchs of
   England, 115–16
William I, King, 118–19
William III of Orange, Prince,
   115–16
William of Orange, 87–89, 90, 103
Willibrord (early missionary), 77
windmills, *8*, 31, 41, *150*
women, status of, 13, 16, 57–60, 79,
   98, 103, 111, 124
work ethic, 5, 19–20, 104, 138, 139,
   140, 141, 145, 151–52
World War I, 125
World War II, 9, 13, 39, 125–35,
   177, 180, 192
   contemporary attitudes about,
     133–34
   cooperation with Nazis, 13, 126–27,
     133–34
   famine, 39, 132, *133*
   Jews, Dutch, extermination of,
     127–30, *128*
   liberation of Holland, 132, 133
   Nazi invasion, 125–26
   postwar economic struggle, 141–43,
     177
   resistance to Nazis, 126, 127,
     130–32, *131*, 133–34
writers, 32–33, 79–80, 105–6, 123,
   129–30, 141, 179–80, 203, 204

Zeeland province, 28, 29, 31, 45, 79,
   82, 89, 90
Zuiderzee region, 25, 42–43, 44
Zutphen, 22, 80
Zwolle, 80